MOE ♥ MANIAX

CONTENTS

D1414041

SPURT!
IT'S HOT INSIDE ME... SO HOT!
ONII-CHAAAAAN!
WE DIDN'T ACTUALLY MEET...
...UNTIL TODAY.
Quest.
TRIANGLE△GUILD

THERE'S JUST... ONE THING...
THAT MAKES US DIFFERENT FROM OTHER PEOPLE...
PRESS
WAAAHH!
AH! AAAAH!
GUH!
SHUDDER
I LOVE ONII-CHAN'S COCK! ♥
MIX IT AROUND MORE AND MORE INSIDE OF CHII! ♥
NNGAH!
SPURT
SPURT

HER EROGENOUS ZONES...
THE POSITIONS SHE LIKES...
I KNOW ALL OF HER LITTLE SEXUAL QUIRKS.
HAAA...
SHUDDER SHUDDER
MY BUTT... FEELS GOOOOD! ♥
SHLUP
SQUELCH
SHLUP
WAAAAAAH! ♥
SQUISH
NOT MY BOOOOBS!
HAA!
HAA...
AHH...! ♥
AND THAT'S BECAUSE ...
I'VE BEEN SEEING HER FOR ALMOST A YEAR NOW.

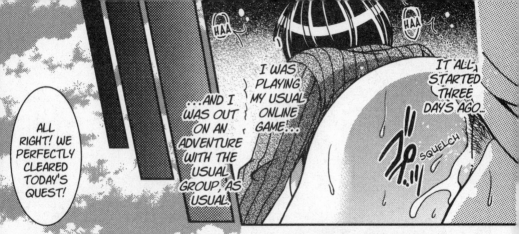

ALL RIGHT! WE PERFECTLY CLEARED TODAY'S QUEST!

...AND I WAS OUT ON AN ADVENTURE WITH THE USUAL GROUP, AS USUAL.

I WAS PLAYING MY USUAL ONLINE GAME!...

IT ALL STARTED THREE DAYS AGO...

HAA

HAA

SQUELCH

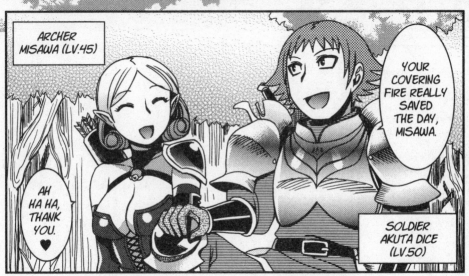

ARCHER MISAWA (LV.45)

YOUR COVERING FIRE REALLY SAVED THE DAY, MISAWA.

AH HA HA, THANK YOU. ♥

SOLDIER AKUTA DICE (LV.50)

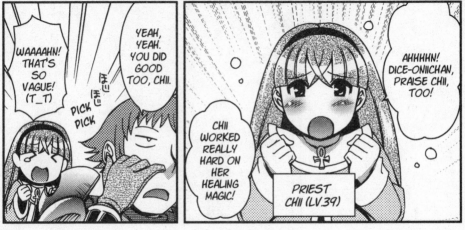

WAAAAHN! THAT'S SO VAGUE! (T_T)

YEAH, YEAH. YOU DID GOOD TOO, CHII.

PICK PICK

CHII WORKED REALLY HARD ON HER HEALING MAGIC!

AHHHHN! DICE-ONIICHAN, PRAISE CHII, TOO!

PRIEST CHII (LV.39)

5

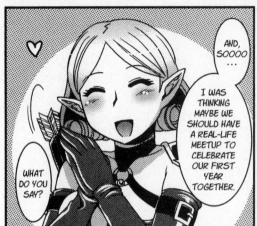

AND, SOOOO...

I WAS THINKING MAYBE WE SHOULD HAVE A REAL-LIFE MEETUP TO CELEBRATE OUR FIRST YEAR TOGETHER.

WHAT DO YOU SAY?

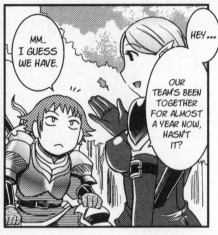

MM... I GUESS WE HAVE.

HEY...

OUR TEAM'S BEEN TOGETHER FOR ALMOST A YEAR NOW, HASN'T IT?

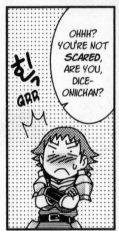

OHHH? YOU'RE NOT *SCARED*, ARE YOU, DICE-ONIICHAN?

QRR

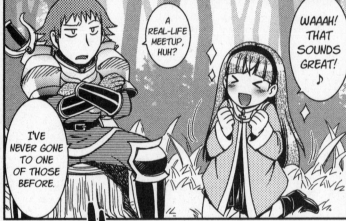

A REAL-LIFE MEETUP, HUH?

WAAAH! THAT SOUNDS GREAT! ♪

I'VE NEVER GONE TO ONE OF THOSE BEFORE.

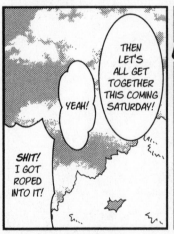

THEN LET'S ALL GET TOGETHER THIS COMING SATURDAY!

YEAH!

SHIT! I GOT ROPED INTO IT!

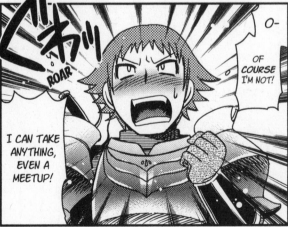

ROAR

I CAN TAKE ANYTHING, EVEN A MEETUP!

O- OF *COURSE* I'M NOT!

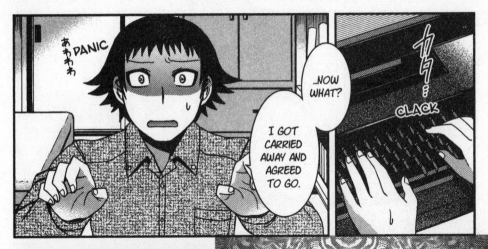

あわわ PANIC

...NOW WHAT?

I GOT CARRIED AWAY AND AGREED TO GO.

CLACK

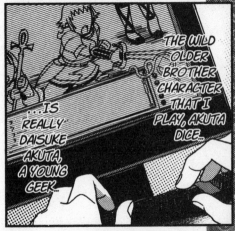

...IS REALLY DAISUKE AKUTA, A YOUNG GEEK...

THE WILD OLDER BROTHER CHARACTER THAT I PLAY, AKUTA DICE...

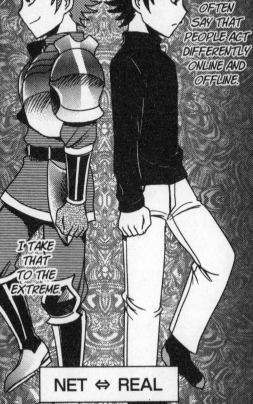

THEY OFTEN SAY THAT PEOPLE ACT DIFFERENTLY ONLINE AND OFFLINE.

I TAKE THAT TO THE EXTREME.

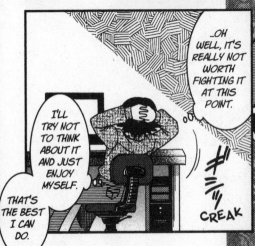

...OH WELL, IT'S REALLY NOT WORTH FIGHTING IT AT THIS POINT.

I'LL TRY NOT TO THINK ABOUT IT AND JUST ENJOY MYSELF.

THAT'S THE BEST I CAN DO.

CREAK

NET ⇔ REAL

THE DAY OF THE MEETUP...
UMM...
GLANCE
GLANCE
I'M PRETTY SURE WE WERE SUPPOSED TO MEET AROUND HERE SOMEWHERE...
!
ARE YOU AKUTA DICE-SAN?
OH... YEAH, I AM.
GOOD, I WAS RIGHT!
I'M MISAWA. NICE TO SEE YOU!
WHOA. MISAWA-SAN'S A BABE!
SAME HERE.
UMM... THEN...
CHII-SAN...
IS...
LOOM
WAAAH?!
STARTLE
AH HA HA. YOU REALLY LIKE THAT, DON'T YOU, CHII-SAN?
SHE DID THAT TO ME JUST A BIT AGO!
...YES?
...I'M LOOKING FORWARD TO TODAY.
OH... YEAH.
ME... TOO.

HMM?
SO YOU YOU TOOK YOUR HANDLE FROM YOUR REAL NAME, DICE-SAN.
THEN I'LL HAVE TO CALL YOU DAISUKE-KUN OFFLINE FROM NOW ON. ♥
WAH.
NO ONE'S CALLED ME BY MY FIRST NAME IN A WHILE. IT'S KINDA EMBAR-RASSING.
THEN BE EMBAR-RASSED! ♥
BUT REALLY, DAISUKE-KUN, YOU'RE SO OVERBEARING IN THE GAME.
YOU'RE USUALLY LIKE THIS...
I TOTALLY DIDN'T EXPECT YOU TO BE SUCH A FINE YOUNG MAN IN PERSON.
SHUT YOUR TRAPS...
...AND FOLLOW ME!
Y-YEAH, BUT A LOT OF PEOPLE...
SHOW THEIR HIDDEN, TRUE SIDES ONLINE, Y'KNOW.
OH..? SO YOU'RE A CLOSET SADIST?
CHATTER CHATTER
N-NO!
THAT'S NOT WHAT I MEANT...
GULP

AHH...
THIS WAS FUN!
YEAH.
WE SHOULD GET TOGETHER AGAIN SOMETIME.
BY THE WAY... ARE YOU SURE YOU'RE OKAY?
I KNOW YOU'RE LOCAL, BUT STILL, TAKING CARE OF CHIRI-CHAN...
DRUNK
YEAH... I'M FINE.
YOUR HOUSE IS PRETTY FAR, AFTER ALL, KUZUMI-SAN.
LET'S CALL IT A NIGHT BEFORE YOU MISS THE LAST TRAIN.
...DAISUKE-KUN.

DO TRY NOT TO TAKE ADVANTAGE OF HER WHILE SHE SLEEPS, OKAY?
LIKE THE BIG BAD WOLF.
WHA?
I'D NEVER DO SOMETHING LIKE THAT!
くすくす
HEH HEH
HA HA, JUST KIDDING.
YOU ARE SO FUN TO TEASE, DAISUKE-KUN.
WELL THEN, GOOD NIGHT.
SEE YOU IN THE GAME!
OH!
はあ
SIGH
MM ...
AND... THERE.
I'LL GET HER SETTLED IN MY FUTON FOR NOW ...
FLUMP
...

...I DIDN'T REALLY TALK TO CHIRI-SAN AT ALL.
SHE'S A GOOD GIRL, TOTALLY UNLIKE HER CHARACTER...
SO I WASN'T REALLY SURE HOW TO DEAL WITH HER...
SIT UP
...NNGH...
CLATTER
HUH...? WHAT IS THIS PLACE?
EEEVERY-THING'S BLURRY. CHII'S CONFUSED...
HUH?
U-UM...
CHIRI-SAN?
!

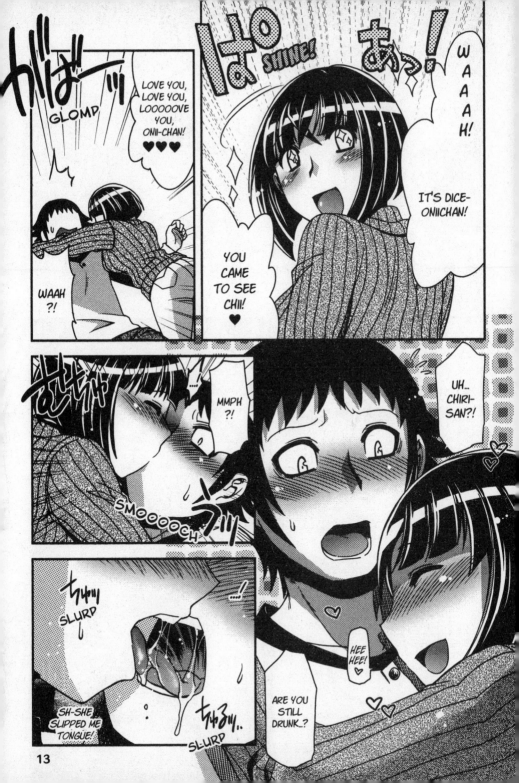

GLOMP

LOVE YOU, LOVE YOU, LOOOOOVE YOU, ONII-CHAN! ♥♥♥

SHINE!

WAAAH!

IT'S DICE-ONIICHAN!

YOU CAME TO SEE CHII! ♥

WAAH?!

MMPH?!

....

SMOOOOCH

UH... CHIRI-SAN?!

SLURP

....

SH-SHE SLIPPED ME TONGUE!

SLURP

ARE YOU STILL DRUNK...?

HEE HEE! ♥

PRESS
MMMWA.
MMMM...
MWA
HEY... ONII-CHAN.
LET'S... FUCK.
LIKE WE ALWAYS DO. ♥
TUG
BWA?!
WAI... HUUUH?!
WHAT DO YOU MEAN, LIKE WE ALWAYS DO?!
HALF YOUR BUTT'S HANGING OUT!
...COME TO THINK OF IT...
SOMETIMES CHII AND I WOULD DO THAT KIND OF THING IN THE IN-GAME CHAT.

HAA
HAA
WE HAD TEXT-BASED PSEUDO SEX...
AS WE KEPT UP THE ACT...
... I STARTED GETTING REALLY TURNED ON BY HER RESPONSES.
AND... CHII...
...ALWAYS STARTED OUT WITH A KISS.
AND THEN...
CHII: HEY... DO... MY BUTT... ♥
TUG
MM... ♥

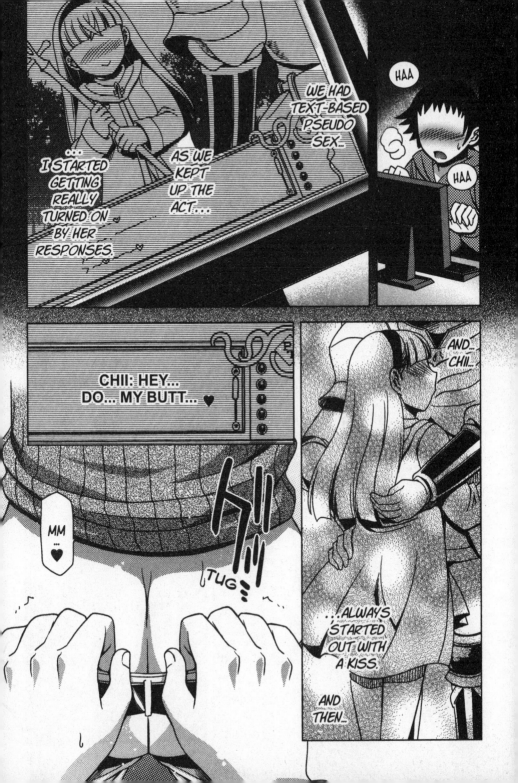

SLIDE!
O-OH? YOU'RE ALREADY SOPPING WET.
DID THAT KISS TURN YOU ON?
TREMBLE
AHHN... IT... DID!
I WANT YOU SO BAD I CAN HARDLY STAND IT, ONII-CHAN...
SHLUP
WAAAAHN!
YOU WANT ME... TO PLAY WITH YOUR ASS THAT BADLY?
YOU REALLY **ARE** A COMPLETE PERVERT, AREN'T YOU?!
SHLUP
WAAAAH! AAHHN!
SHLUP
SHLUP
SHLUP

HAAAA...
AHH.
SLURP
HAAAA...
MY BUTT... FEELS GOOOOD! ♥
SLURP
SLURP
SHUDDER!
...THIS ISN'T CHIRI-SAN RIGHT NOW. IT'S CHII.
GASP
PRESS!
SQUELCH
SQUELCH
I KNOW EXACTLY...
AH.
...HOW TO DEAL WITH CHII.
AAHH.
SQUELCH
HAA!

JIGGLE!
AAAAHH?!
WAAAAAAH! ♥
NOT MY BOOOOBS!
SQUISH
THEY FEEL TOO GOOD ...
I'M GONNA ...
SQUISH SQUISH
SHUDDER!
SQUEEEEEEEZE
AH!
AAAAAAAAHHHHH...!
SQUIRT

HAA.
HAA...
AAHH...♥
HA...♥
SHUDDER
HEY... ONII... CHAN.
I... CAN'T TAKE IT ANYMORE.
...!
I WANT YOU TO THRUST...
RIGHT INTO ME FROM BEHIND! ♥♥
SPREAD

O-OKAY.
KA-CHINK KA-CHINK
SQUELCH
BUT DON'T COME CRYING TO ME ... LATER!
AH.
HA ...
WAAAAAAH!
THRUST!
AH!
AH.
FWAP
AHHHN!
NNGAH!
FWAP FWAP
SQUELCH
AMAZING... HER INNER FOLDS ARE CLINGING TO ME.
MY GROIN'S TINGLING!

THRUST
HAAAAAH!
AHH!
AH!
IT'S... BUMPING UP DEEP INSIDE ME!
THRUST
THRUST
I LOVE ONII-CHAN'S COCK! ♥
THRUST!
THRUST!
MIX IT AROUND MORE AND MORE INSIDE OF CHII! ♥
THRUST!
UH... GH!
I'M GONNA COME, CHII!
THRUST
BE SURE TO TAKE IT ALL!

NNGAH!
IT'S HOT INSIDE ME... SO HOT!
SPURT
SPLURT
SPURT
ONII-CHAAAAAN!

...MMM...
MOR-NING?
CHIRP
CHIRP
...OH YEAH, LAST NIGHT...
GASP
...CHIRI-SAN AND I DID SOMETHING OUTRA-GEOUS...!
スー…ッ
SLIDE
SIZZLE
OH...
SHE'S...
...MAKING BREAK-FAST.

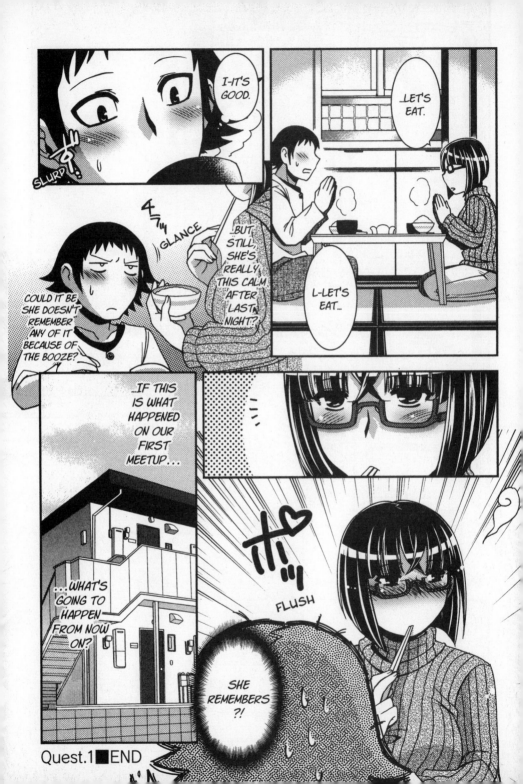

I-IT'S GOOD.

SLURP

...LET'S EAT.

L-LET'S EAT...

GLANCE

...BUT STILL, SHE'S REALLY THIS CALM AFTER LAST NIGHT?

COULD IT BE SHE DOESN'T REMEMBER ANY OF IT BECAUSE OF THE BOOZE?

...IF THIS IS WHAT HAPPENED ON OUR FIRST MEETUP...

...WHAT'S GOING TO HAPPEN FROM NOW ON?

FLUSH

SHE REMEMBERS?!

Quest.1 ■END

LET'S GO OVER THE PLAN.
I'LL CHARGE THE ENEMY HEAD ON AND DRAW ITS ATTENTION.
WHILE I DO THAT, MISAWA, YOU PROVIDE COVERING FIRE FROM THE LEFT REAR.
AND CHII, YOU WAIT ON STANDBY AND BUFF US FROM THE RIGHT REAR.
LET'S GO!
OKAY!
GOT IT!
CHARGE!
SLIDE
GRAB
HUH?

WAAAAAAH!
LIFT
OH, NO! THERE'S ANOTHER ENEMY BEHIND US!
WHOOSH
SLASH
Quest.2
TRIANGLE△GUILD
TRIANGLE△GUILD

...ARE YOU HURT?
OH ...
N-NO...
WE'LL FALL BACK FOR NOW.
LET'S GO BACK TO TOWN.
...
...SORRY, ONII-CHAN.
IT'S ALL CHII'S FAULT THAT WE FAILED THE QUEST.
WELL... YOU KNOW...
DON'T WORRY ABOUT IT.
THESE THINGS HAPPEN.
PAT
MM...
...I'M GOING OUT TOMORROW, SO I'M DONE FOR TODAY.
GOOD NIGHT...
FWISH
CHII HAS LOGGED OUT.

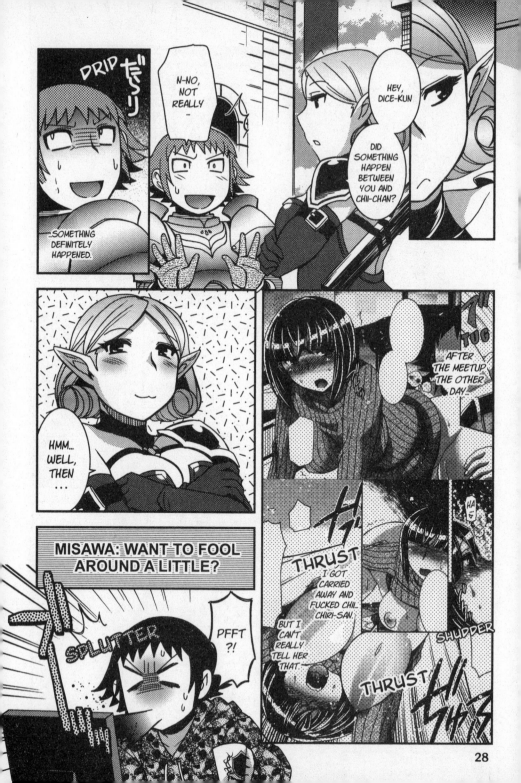

DRIP

...SOMETHING DEFINITELY HAPPENED.

N-NO, NOT REALLY...

HEY, DICE-KUN

DID SOMETHING HAPPEN BETWEEN YOU AND CHII-CHAN?

HMM... WELL, THEN...

AFTER THE MEETUP THE OTHER DAY...

TUG

MISAWA: WANT TO FOOL AROUND A LITTLE?

SPLUTTER

PFFT ?!

THRUST

HA HA

I GOT CARRIED AWAY AND FUCKED CHII... CHIRI-SAN.

BUT I CAN'T REALLY TELL HER THAT.

SHUDDER

THRUST

28

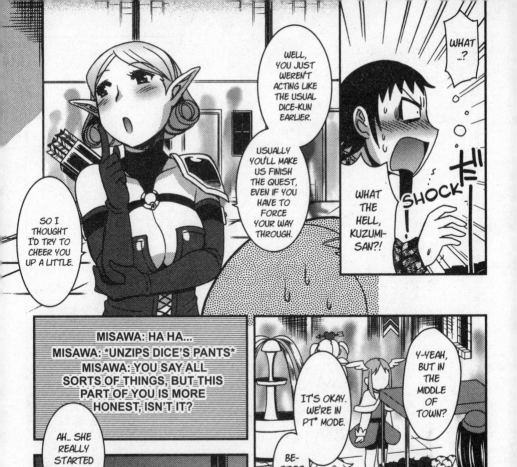

SO I THOUGHT I'D TRY TO CHEER YOU UP A LITTLE.

WELL, YOU JUST WEREN'T ACTING LIKE THE USUAL DICE-KUN EARLIER.

USUALLY YOU'LL MAKE US FINISH THE QUEST, EVEN IF YOU HAVE TO FORCE YOUR WAY THROUGH.

WHAT ...?

SHOCK!!

WHAT THE HELL, KUZUMI-SAN?!

MISAWA: HA HA...
MISAWA: *UNZIPS DICE'S PANTS*
MISAWA: YOU SAY ALL SORTS OF THINGS, BUT THIS PART OF YOU IS MORE HONEST, ISN'T IT?

AH... SHE REALLY STARTED DOING IT.

I GUESS I'LL HAVE TO PLAY ALONG.

CREAK

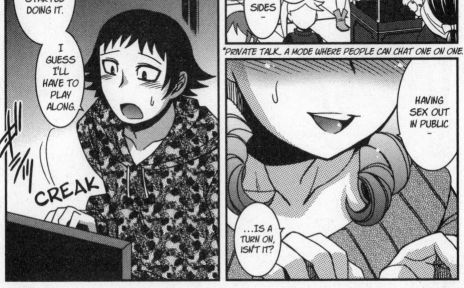

IT'S OKAY. WE'RE IN PT* MODE.

BE-SIDES...

Y-YEAH, BUT IN THE MIDDLE OF TOWN?

*PRIVATE TALK... A MODE WHERE PEOPLE CAN CHAT ONE ON ONE.

HAVING SEX OUT IN PUBLIC...

...IS A TURN ON, ISN'T IT?

29

NN... HAA.
NNNGH...
HA... AH.
SHLUP
SHLUP
SHLUP
SQUEEZE
SHLUP
PRESS
YOUR... COCK IS...
SHLUP
SHLUP
AMAZING! ♥
I'M... COMING.
COMING!
SHUDDER SHUDDER
AH.
SHUDDER
AHH!
...!!

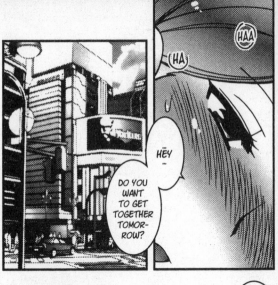

DO YOU WANT TO GET TOGETHER TOMOR- ROW?

HEY ...

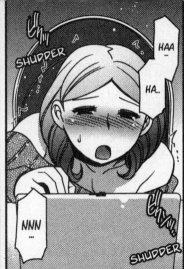

SHUDDER

HAA ...

HAA ...

HA...

NNN ...

SHUDDER

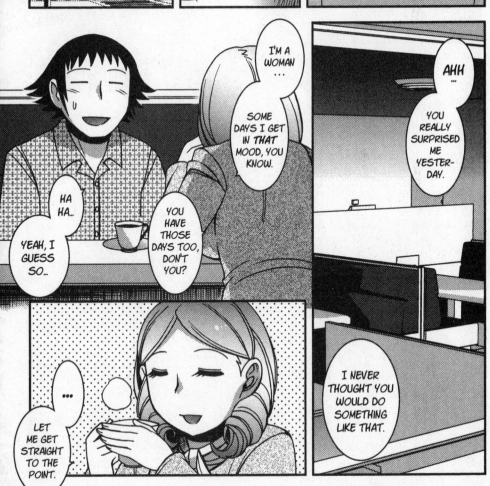

I'M A WOMAN ...

SOME DAYS I GET IN *THAT* MOOD, YOU KNOW.

HA HA...

YEAH, I GUESS SO...

YOU HAVE THOSE DAYS TOO, DON'T YOU?

AHH ...

YOU REALLY SURPRISED ME YESTER- DAY.

I NEVER THOUGHT YOU WOULD DO SOMETHING LIKE THAT.

...

LET ME GET STRAIGHT TO THE POINT.

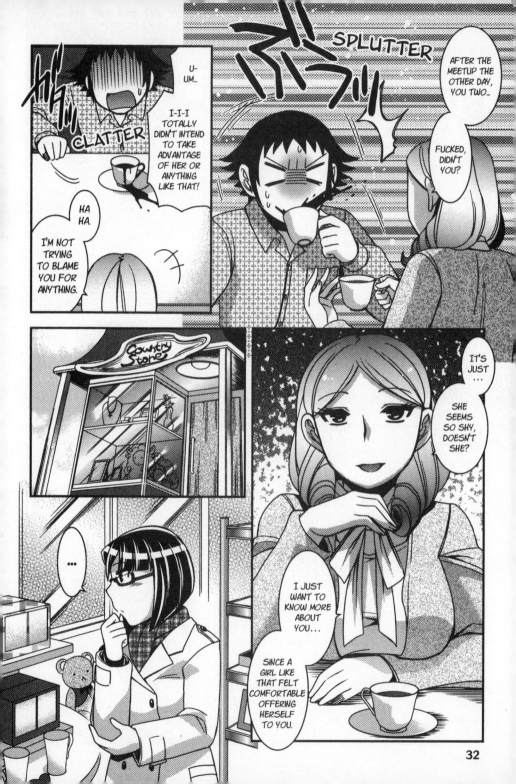

SPLUTTER

AFTER THE MEETUP THE OTHER DAY, YOU TWO...

FUCKED, DIDN'T YOU?

U-UM...

I-I-I TOTALLY DIDN'T INTEND TO TAKE ADVANTAGE OF HER OR ANYTHING LIKE THAT!

CLATTER

HA HA.

I'M NOT TRYING TO BLAME YOU FOR ANYTHING.

Country Store

...

IT'S JUST ...

SHE SEEMS SO SHY, DOESN'T SHE?

I JUST WANT TO KNOW MORE ABOUT YOU...

SINCE A GIRL LIKE THAT FELT COMFORTABLE OFFERING HERSELF TO YOU.

32

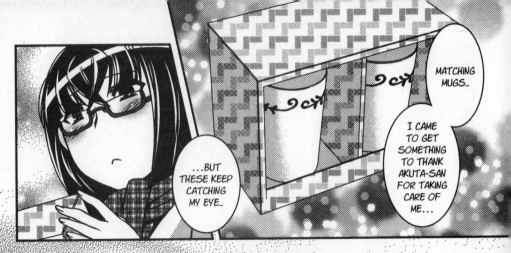

MATCHING MUGS...

I CAME TO GET SOMETHING TO THANK AKUTA-SAN FOR TAKING CARE OF ME...

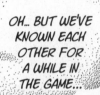

...BUT THESE KEEP CATCHING MY EYE...

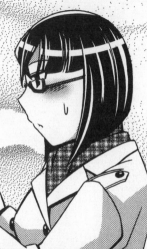

OH... BUT WE'VE KNOWN EACH OTHER FOR A WHILE IN THE GAME...

...SO THEY'RE MATCHING TO SAY "I'M LOOKING FORWARD TO THE FUTURE"...

...WE JUST MET IN PERSON THE OTHER DAY.

SUDDENLY SENDING HIM SOMETHING LIKE THIS... WOULD CAUSE PROBLEMS.

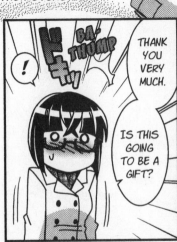

BA-THUMP

!

THANK YOU VERY MUCH.

IS THIS GOING TO BE A GIFT?

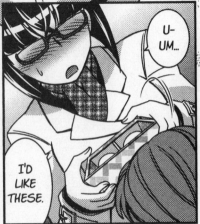

U-UM...

I'D LIKE THESE.

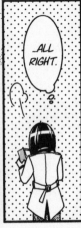

...ALL RIGHT.

...YES...
WE WERE JUST SUPPOSED TO BE...
...HAVING TEA.
MMMPH... ♥
SUCK
MM!
SLURP SUUUCK
MMMHA... ♥
WAAH
WHAT DID I SCREW UP...
SHUDDER!
HA!
SUCK ♥
SLURP
SHUDDER!
SUUCK ♥
TO HAVE IT TURN OUT LIKE THIS?!

MWA ...
YOUR COCK IS SO MUCH BIGGER THAN I IMAGINED.
I'M HAVING A HARD TIME TENDING TO IT. ♥
HAAAA!
HAMPH
WA... AH!
KUZUMI-SAN, DON'T.
SUCK
MM
IF YOU DO THAT..!
MMPH
MM ♥
SUCK
SUCK
SUCK SUCK
HA... UH.
AH.
LAP
LAP
LIIIICK
UHHH!

FLUMP
AAAH ?!
RUB
N-NO WAY!
RUB
HER BOOBS ARE COMPLETELY SURROUNDING IT?!
SQUISH
HEY... DID SHE DO THIS FOR YOU?
BETWEEN HER AND ME...
WHICH OF OUR BREASTS FELT BETTER?
SQUISH
SQUISH
SQUISH
I-I...
CAN'T POSSIBLY ...
COMPARE THEM!
SQUEEZE
AAAAHHH!
SQUEEZE

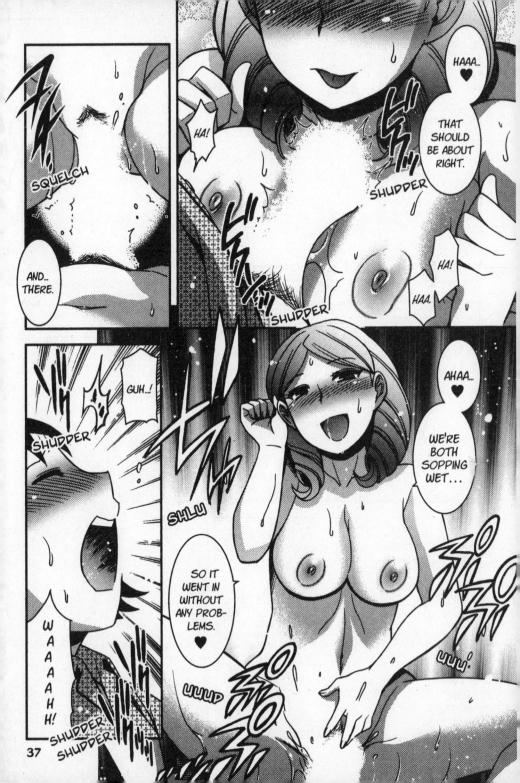

SQUELCH

AND... THERE.

HA!

HAAA... ♥

THAT SHOULD BE ABOUT RIGHT.

SHUDDER

HA!

HAA.

SHUDDER

SHUDDER

GUH...!

WAAAAHH!

SHUDDER SHUDDER

SHLU

SO IT WENT IN WITHOUT ANY PROBLEMS. ♥

AHAA... ♥

WE'RE BOTH SOPPING WET...

UUUP

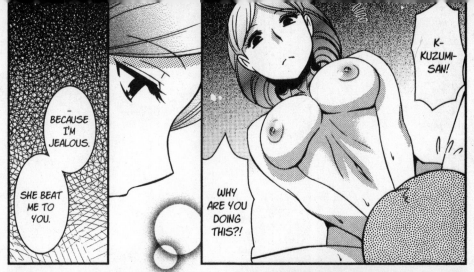

...BECAUSE I'M JEALOUS.

SHE BEAT ME TO YOU.

WHY ARE YOU DOING THIS?!

K-KUZUMI-SAN!

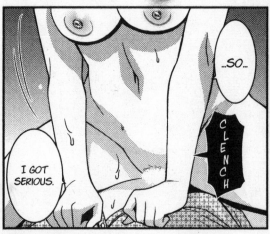

...SO...

I GOT SERIOUS.

C L E N C H

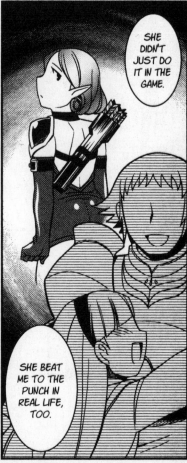

SHE DIDN'T JUST DO IT IN THE GAME.

SHE BEAT ME TO THE PUNCH IN REAL LIFE, TOO.

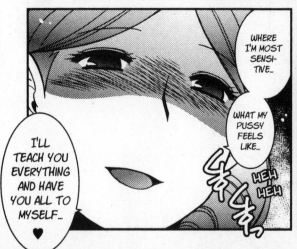

WHERE I'M MOST SENSITIVE...

WHAT MY PUSSY FEELS LIKE...

HEH HEH

I'LL TEACH YOU EVERYTHING AND HAVE YOU ALL TO MYSELF... ♥

38

WHA?
SHE'S DOING THIS BECAUSE OF THAT?!
I'M... GOING TO START MOVING NOW.
MMPH ...
SQUELCH
SQUELCH
SQUELCH
UHH. ♥
NNGAH!
AH! ♥
DAISUKE-KUN.
SQUELCH
MY PUSSY ...
I'LL MAKE YOU CUM AND CUM AND REMEMBER HOW I FEEL... ♥
SQUELCH
SQUELCH SQUELCH
...!
BA-THUMP
BA-THUMP
BA-THUMP
...WHAT DO YOU MEAN YOU WANT ME ALL TO YOURSELF?
I'M... NOT A THING!
BA-THUMP
BA-THUMP

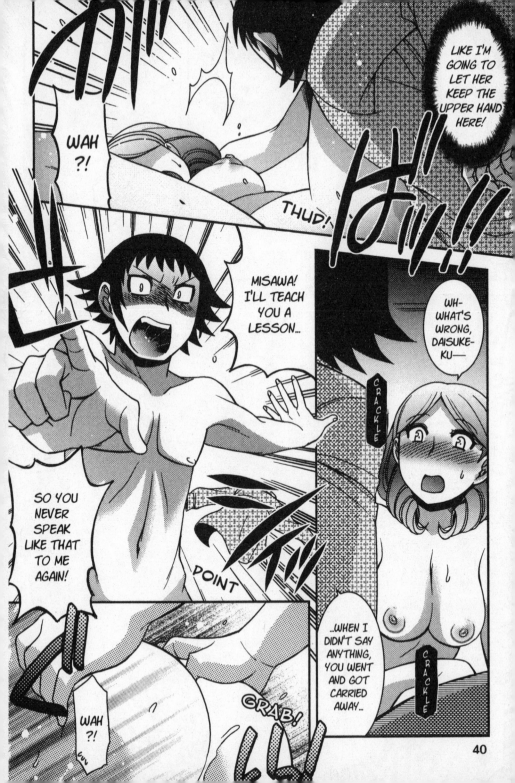

LIKE I'M GOING TO LET HER KEEP THE UPPER HAND HERE!

WAH?!

THUD!

MISAWA! I'LL TEACH YOU A LESSON...

SO YOU NEVER SPEAK LIKE THAT TO ME AGAIN!

POINT

WH- WHAT'S WRONG, DAISUKE- KU—

CRACKLE

...WHEN I DIDN'T SAY ANYTHING, YOU WENT AND GOT CARRIED AWAY...

CRACKLE

WAH?!

GRAB!

WAH!
AH!
IF YOU'RE... THAT ROUGH ...
YOU'LL BREAK ME!
THRUST!
THRUST
THRUST!
LIKE YOU'D EVER BREAK THAT EASILY!
THRUST!
I'M GONNA POUND INTO YOU!
WAAAAAH!
HAA...!
THRUST
THRUST
RUB
AH... AH!
AHHHH!
RUB RUB
TREMBLE
NOOO... NOOO...
MY WOMB... I'M WEAK...
♥ TO THAT! ♥
TREMBLE TREMBLE

OH? YOU'RE COMING ?!
DO IT!
I'LL PUMP YOU FULL OF SOME-THING SO HOT
IT BURNS YOU UP!
WAAA ...
AH.
SPURT!
SPURT!
SPLURT
NNGAA-AAHH!

HAAA...
YOU REALLY ARE A CLOSET SADIST, DAISUKE-KUN.
THAT SORT OF SUDDEN TRANSFORMATION MIGHT EVEN BE RARER THAN RARE EQUIPMENT. ♥
SIGH
ほっ…
PLEASE DON'T ADMIRE IT...
...IT'S ALL KIND OF FUZZY.
APPARENTLY I SWITCHED TO MY GAME PERSONA.
THERE WERE SOME SIGNS OF THAT HAPPENING WHEN I FUCKED CHIRI-SAN TOO. THEN...
THAT...
THRUST
TREMBLE
IS THE REAL ME?
POINT
GRAB
...HEY! WHY DID YOU GRAB MY ARM LIKE THAT?!
ぎゅー♥
HUG
AWW, COME ON! WE DID JUST FUCK LIKE BUNNIES, AFTER ALL! ♥

TREMBLE
...!
TREMBLE
CRASH!
!
DASH
WAS THAT...
...CHIRI-SAN?!

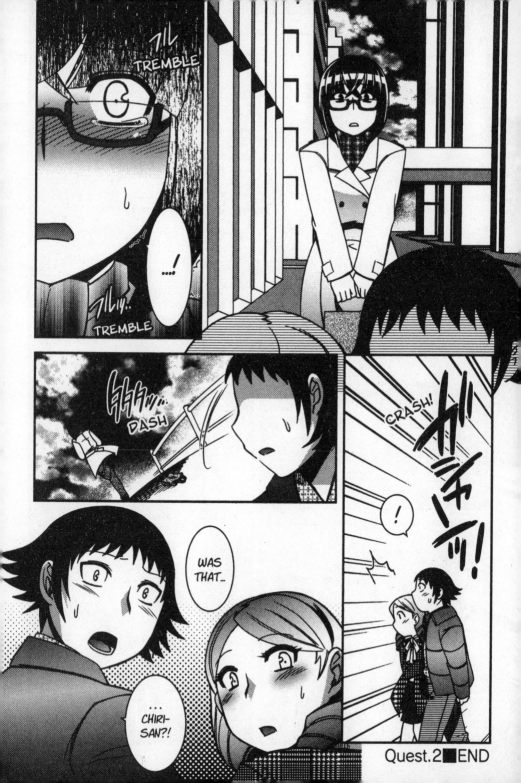

Quest.2■END

KA-CHAK
CREAK
SHUT
...
FWISH
HAA...
CREAK

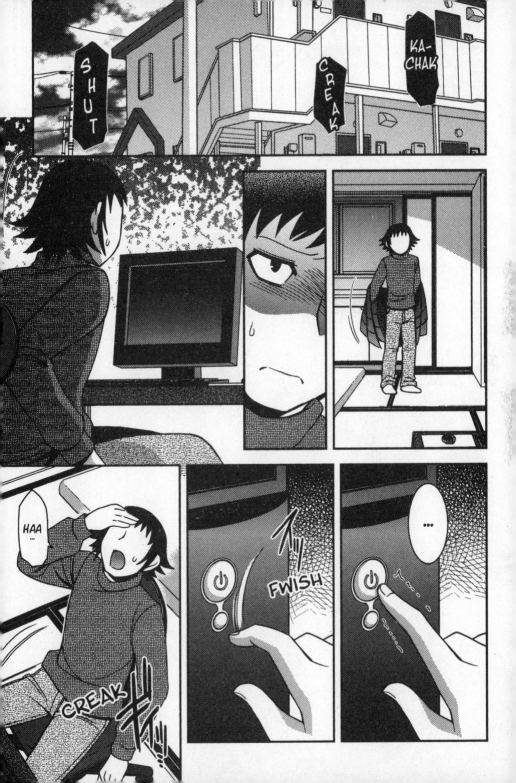

EVER SINCE...
...CHIRI-SAN SAW ME...
...WITH KUZUMI-SAN THE OTHER DAY...
TRIANGLE△GUILD
Final Quest
I...
...HAVEN'T LOGGED ON TO THE GAME...

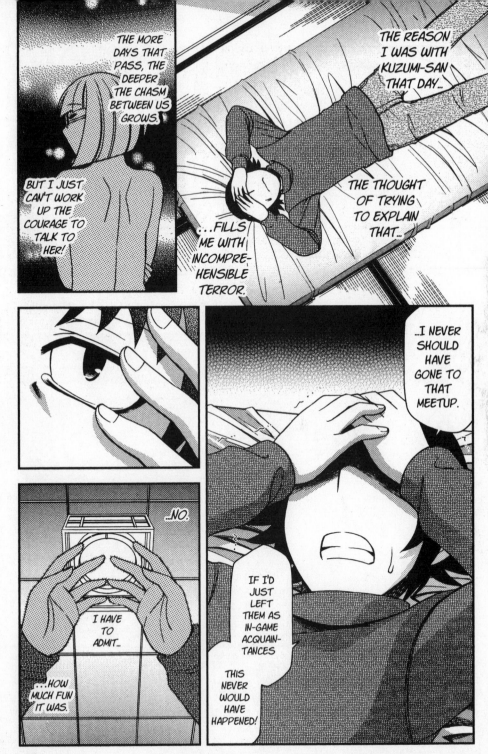

THE MORE DAYS THAT PASS, THE DEEPER THE CHASM BETWEEN US GROWS.

BUT I JUST CAN'T WORK UP THE COURAGE TO TALK TO HER!

THE REASON I WAS WITH KUZUMI-SAN THAT DAY...

...FILLS ME WITH INCOMPREHENSIBLE TERROR.

THE THOUGHT OF TRYING TO EXPLAIN THAT...

...I NEVER SHOULD HAVE GONE TO THAT MEETUP.

...NO.

I HAVE TO ADMIT...

...HOW MUCH FUN IT WAS.

IF I'D JUST LEFT THEM AS IN-GAME ACQUAINTANCES

THIS NEVER WOULD HAVE HAPPENED!

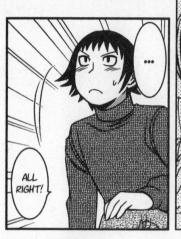

...

ALL RIGHT!

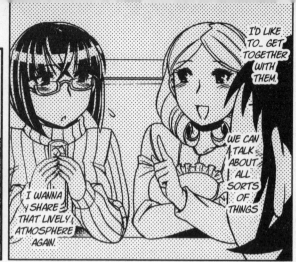

I WANNA SHARE THAT LIVELY ATMOSPHERE AGAIN.

I'D LIKE TO... GET TOGETHER WITH THEM.

WE CAN TALK ABOUT ALL SORTS OF THINGS

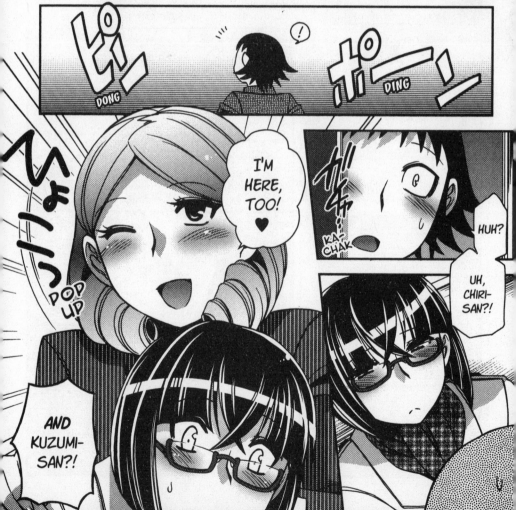

DONG

!

DING

POP UP

I'M HERE, TOO! ♥

KA-CHAK

HUH?

UH, CHIRI-SAN?!

AND KUZUMI-SAN?!

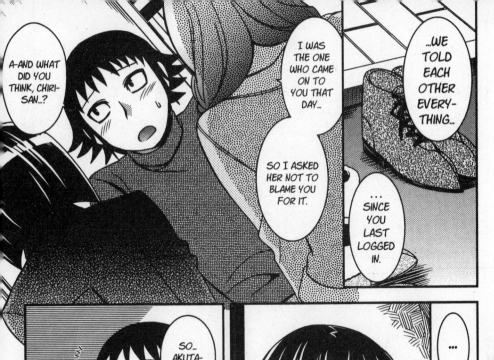

A-AND WHAT DID YOU THINK, CHIRI-SAN...?

I WAS THE ONE WHO CAME ON TO YOU THAT DAY...

SO I ASKED HER NOT TO BLAME YOU FOR IT.

...WE TOLD EACH OTHER EVERY-THING...

... SINCE YOU LAST LOGGED IN.

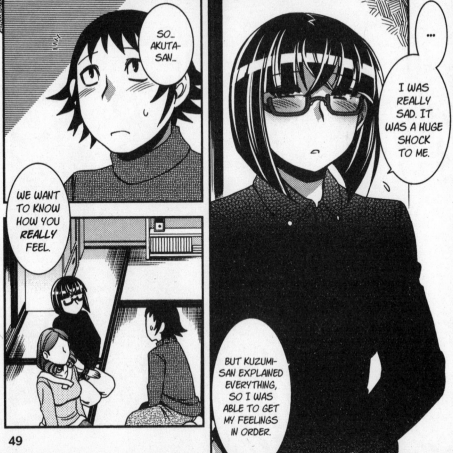

SO... AKUTA-SAN...

WE WANT TO KNOW HOW YOU *REALLY* FEEL.

...

I WAS REALLY SAD. IT WAS A HUGE SHOCK TO ME.

BUT KUZUMI-SAN EXPLAINED EVERYTHING, SO I WAS ABLE TO GET MY FEELINGS IN ORDER.

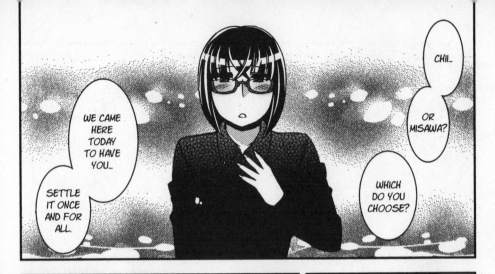

WE CAME HERE TODAY TO HAVE YOU...

SETTLE IT ONCE AND FOR ALL.

CHII...

OR MISAWA?

WHICH DO YOU CHOOSE?

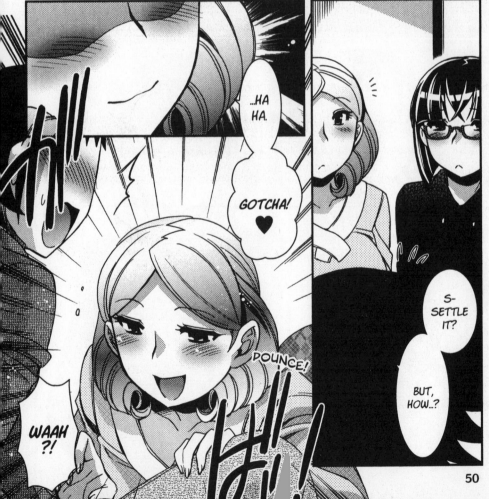

...HA HA.

GOTCHA! ♥

POUNCE!

WAAH ?!

S-SETTLE IT?

BUT, HOW...?

H-H-HEY!
WHAT ARE YOU DOING, KUZUMI-SAN?!
WH-WHAT HE SAID!
JUST JUMPING HIM LIKE THAT!
KA-CHINK
KA-CHINK
HEH
THAT JUST WON'T DO, CHIRI-CHAN.
OUR BATTLE HAS ALREADY STARTED.
THE EARLY BIRD GETS THE WORM, AFTER ALL. ♥
SPROING♥
OKAY!
GET NICE AND BIG FOR ME! ♥
RUB
RUB RUB
AH... AHH!
GUH...!
HUDDER
SHLUP SHLUP
SHLUP

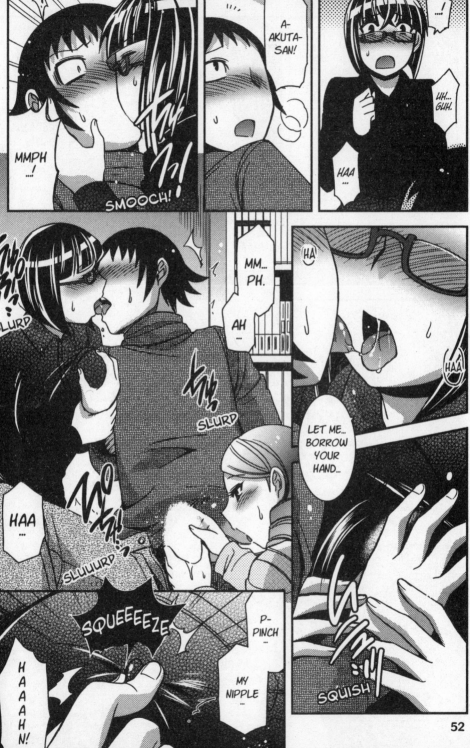

MMPH...!

SMOOCH!

A-AKUTA-SAN!

...!

UH... GUH.

HAA...

MM... PH.

AH...

SLURP

SLURP

HA'

HAA

HAA...

SLUUURD

LET ME... BORROW YOUR HAND...

SQUEEEEEZE

P-PINCH... MY NIPPLE...

HAAAHN!

SQUISH

...DO YOU REMEMBER?
HAA
HAA
ONE YEAR AGO...
I WAS JUST LOOKING FOR A PRIEST.
WANT TO GO ON A QUEST WITH ME?
I'D JUST STARTED PLAYING AND HAD NO IDEA WHAT I WAS DOING...
AND YOU HELPED ME OUT...
YOU WERE A BIT FRIGHTENING AT FIRST...
AKUTA DICE: THANKS FOR YOUR SUPPORT JUST NOW.
AKUTA DICE: ...THIS IS KINDA
MBARRASSING TO SAY IN CHAT,
ET'S SWITCH TO P.T. ^_^
BUT THEN I REALIZED THAT YOU WERE REALLY A NICE PERSON.
I'VE ALWAYS IMAGINED WHAT SORT OF PERSON ...
... WOULD PLAY SUCH A CHARACTER.

SO, AKUTA-SAN... NO...
DAISUKE-SAN, FOR YOU...
SLIDE
CHII WON'T LOSE...
...TO MISAWA-ONEECHAN!
WHA ?!
SHUDDER
AHA! YOUR BALLS ARE SO HEAVY! ♥
BOUNCE
BOUNCE
TODAY CHII WILL MAKE YOU COME...
... UNTIL YOU CAN'T COME ANY MORE... OKAY?
HAAMPH

NN NN ♥
...!
SHE'S... ROLLING MY BALLS AROUND...
IN HER MOUTH...
WITH HER TONGUE!
SLURP
MMMPH ♥
SLURP
SUCK
AHHN!
I CAN DO THAT, TOO!
TUG
MMMPH ...
SLURP
NN.
HAA ...
SLURP
SLURP
NO... WAY.
YOU TOO, KUZUMI-SAN?
AHH...!
SHUDDER!
MMHAA ...
THE MORE I SUCK ON IT...
THE MORE PRECUM COMES FLOWING OUT... ♥
LIIIIIICK
MMM ... ♥

I'LL MAKE YOU GET EVEN WETTER.
TAKE THAT! ♥
GUH ?!
SQUISH
AH!
CHII CAN DO THAT, TOO!
THERE!
HAAA!
SQUISH
TH- THIS IS BAD!
SHLUP
SHLUP
I'M LOSING MY GRIP!
I'M NOT GONNA BE ABLE TO THINK OF ANYTHING BUT CUMMING!
SHLUP
SQUISH
SQUISH
GUH... AH.
HAA...!
SHLUP

OKAY!
TIME FOR A BIT OF A BREAK.
GUUH... ?!
SHLUP!
WAS IT SO GOOD THAT IT MADE YOU FORGET?
THIS... IS A BATTLE WHERE WE'LL GIVE YOU OUR ALL.
NOW...
WHICH SHEATH IS MORE FITTING...
JIGGLE
...FOR YOUR SWORD?
GUH...
AH...
HA
HAA
I-I...

NOT ONLY AM I ABOUT TO EXPLODE FROM STOPPING JUST BEFORE I WAS ABOUT TO COME...
SHLUP♥
BUT... HAVING THOSE DRIPPING WET PUSSIES THRUST RIGHT IN FRONT OF ME...
TWITCH
I CAN'T KEEP MY WITS ABOUT ME...
TWITCH
COME ON... ONII-CHAN...
HURRY UP AND PLAY WITH ME! ♥
...IT WOULD BE SHAMEFUL FOR A MAN TO TURN DOWN SUCH AN INVITATION.
STAND UP
SNAP
CHII!
GRAB!
...AND MISAWA!

I'LL HAVE MY FILL OF BOTH OF YOU AT ONCE!
THRUST!
WAAAAAHH!
AH!
I-IT'S ...
THRUST
IN MY BUUUUTTT!
THRUST
THRUST
HONESTLY... YOU REALLY LOVE ANAL, DON'T YOU, CHII?
YOU'RE CLINGING TO ME EVEN TIGHTER THAN YOU WERE BEFORE.
YOU...
... PERVERTED LITTLE MASOCHIST SLUT!
THRUST!
WAAAAHH!

WAAAAH!
Y-YOUR FINGERS! ♥
SHLUP
SHLUP
SHLUP
THEY'RE GRINDING AGAINST MY G-SPOT... ♥
GRINDING AND GRINDING! ♥
YOU SAID YOU WERE WEAK TO THAT, DIDN'T YOU, MISAWA?
AH
SHLUP
HAAA
SHLUP
SHLUP
I'LL TOP YOU THOROUGHLY ON THE NEXT GO...
...SO JUST SQUIRT AND WAIT YOUR TURN!
GRIND
SQUIIIIRT
WAH... AAAHHH!
I'M COMING!
I'M COOOOOMING!

HA! A CONSE-CUTIVE ATTACK!
THRUST
NNGAH.
FWAP
AH!
FWAP
WAAAAH?!
WAAAAH!
FWAP
ONII... CHAAAAN!
SHUDDER
FILL... CHII'S DIRTY BUTT...
THRUST
THRUST THRUST
WITH YOUR HOT, STEAMING MILK..!
ALL RIGHT...
COME LIKE YOU'RE GONNA GET PREGNANT THROUGH YOUR ASS!
THRUST
AAAAAHH!
COME LIKE CRAZY!
SHUDDER
SHUDDER
SHUDDER
AH!
WAAAAAAAHHH!
SHUDDER
SHUDDER

HAA!
AH!
WAAAAAHN!
AHHN, DAI... SUKE-KUN!
NO... POUNDING INTO MY WOMB!
THRUST
THRUST
THRUST
WAAAAAH!
THRUST
ONII-CHAN!
THRUST
THRUST
THRUST
THRUST
CHII'S... GONNA COME!
WAAH?!
SQUELCH
AH... AHH!
SQUELCH
SQUELCH
IT'S...
RUBBING AGAINST MY CLIT!
TREMBLE
TREMBLE
TREMBLE

GUH... I'M COMING.
WAAAAH... AHH!
PULL
I'LL MARK YOUR SKIN ALL OVER!
HAAAA-AHHHH!
SPUUUURT
SPUUUURT
SPUUUURT
SO, TONIGHT ...
CHII-CHAN AND I WILL HEAD OVER TO YOUR PLACE. ♥
WHA?
YOU'RE GONNA DO THAT AGAIN?!

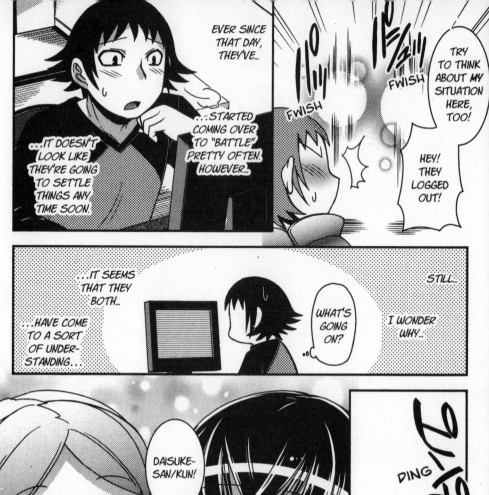

EVER SINCE THAT DAY, THEY'VE...

...STARTED COMING OVER TO "BATTLE" PRETTY OFTEN. HOWEVER...

...IT DOESN'T LOOK LIKE THEY'RE GOING TO SETTLE THINGS ANY TIME SOON.

FWISH

FWISH

TRY TO THINK ABOUT MY SITUATION HERE, TOO!

HEY! THEY LOGGED OUT!

...IT SEEMS THAT THEY BOTH...

...HAVE COME TO A SORT OF UNDER-STANDING...

WHAT'S GOING ON?

STILL...

I WONDER WHY...

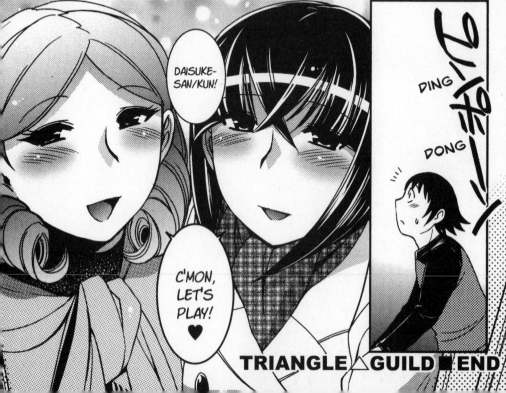

DAISUKE-SAN/KUN!

C'MON, LET'S PLAY! ♥

DING

DONG

TRIANGLE △ GUILD ■ END

IF THEY WERE ALL FPS PLAYERS ...
OKAY!
LET'S RACK UP A HIGH KILL COUNT! ♡
PLOP
KA-BOOM
OH, I'M SORRY.
I MESSED UP MY AIM.
GRUMBLE ブス
ブス GRUMBLE
YOU DID THAT ON PURPOSE, DIDN'T YOU?
BWA HA HA HA HA HA HA HA HA HA!
GOTTA TAKE OUT THE TRASH!
BLAM
BLAM BLAM BLAM BLAM
BLAM BLAM BLAM

MOE-MANIAX

INTERNET GAMER,COSTUME PLAYER,BOYS LOVE-LOVER,
ANIMATION FAN,DRUNKEN OFFICE LADY,BOYS IN GIRLY-COSTUME,
AND SEXY MASSAGE MASTER.CHOOSE YOUR FAVORITE ONE!

presented by
AYA HINASE

THUD

HELLO! THIS IS YANERE FREIGHT.

I'D LIKE YOU TO ACCEPT A PACKAGE FOR YOUR NEIGHBOR...

COM-ING!

IT'S FROM "COSPE"?

THAT COMPANY'S WELL-KNOWN FOR MAKING COSPLAY OUTFITS.

COULD IT BE FOR THE COSPLAY EVENT THIS WEEKEND?

COSPE

U-UM...

CLACK CLACK CLACK

OH!

I USUALLY ONLY SAY "HELLO" TO HER, SO I DON'T REALLY KNOW WHAT SHE'S LIKE.

..MORNING.

I'M PRETTY SURE THERE'S A WOMAN BY THE NAME OF MOMOI-SAN LIVING NEXT DOOR...

GOOD MORNING.

MOMOI-SAN!

KA-CHAK

SHE'S HOME!

BUT SHE'S GOT A PRETTY NICE BODY...

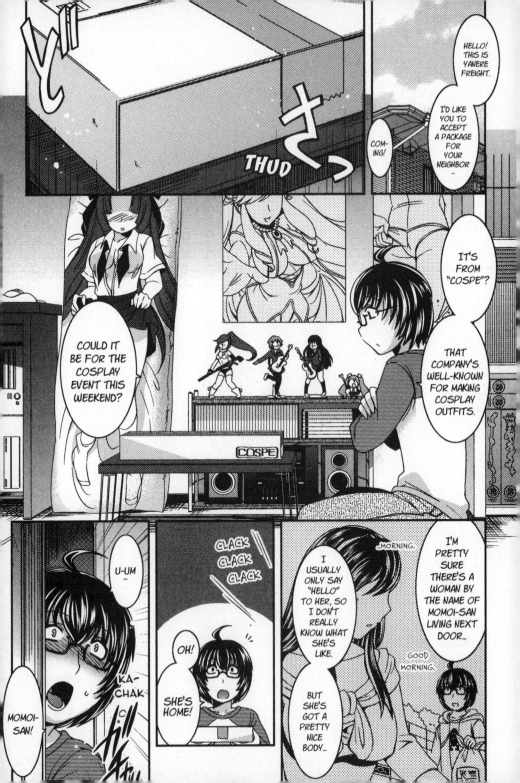

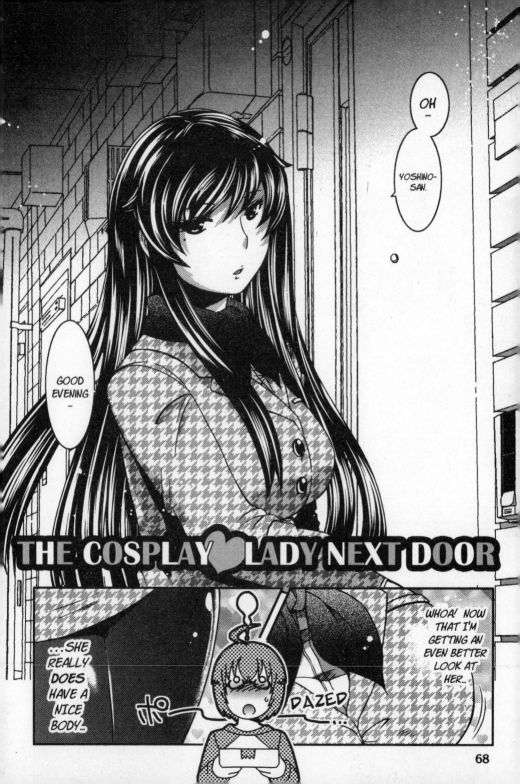

THE COSPLAY ♥ LADY NEXT DOOR

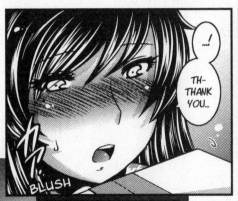

TH-THANK YOU...

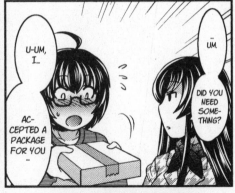

...UM.

U-UM, I...

DID YOU NEED SOMETHING?

AC-CEPTED A PACKAGE FOR YOU...

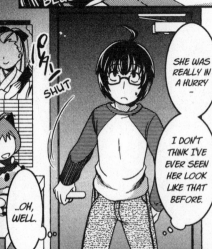

SHE WAS REALLY IN A HURRY...

I DON'T THINK I'VE EVER SEEN HER LOOK LIKE THAT BEFORE.

SHUT

...OH, WELL.

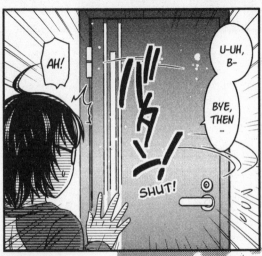

AH!

U-UH, B-

BYE, THEN...

SHUT!

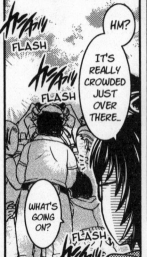

FLASH

HM?

IT'S REALLY CROWDED JUST OVER THERE...

FLASH

WHAT'S GOING ON?

FLASH

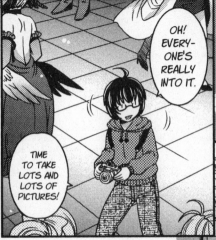

OH! EVERY-ONE'S REALLY INTO IT.

TIME TO TAKE LOTS AND LOTS OF PICTURES!

SUNDAY...

!
THAT'S A CHARACTER FROM VENUS SABER, ONE OF THIS SEASON'S LATE-NIGHT SHOWS!
FLASH
FLASH
WOW... SHE'S GOT THE SAME PROPORTIONS AS THE ORIGINAL...
FLASH
I'LL JUST GET A PICTURE FROM THE SIDE HERE...
FLASH
FLASH
SNAP
SNAP
SNAP

SNAP
...?
HUH? I'VE...
SEEN HER SOME-WHERE BEFORE.
FLASH
WAH!
WHOOSH
WAH! THAT WIND!
...!
M-
~~~~~!
MOMOI-SAN?!
~~~~~

AH!
DASH!
WAIT... MOMOI-SAN!
CLAMOR
CLAMOR
PLEASE, WAIT!
SHOVE
SHUT!
CHANGING ROOM
!
...I GOT CARRIED AWAY AND RAN INSIDE AFTER HER...
PANT
PANT
B-BUT NOW WHAT DO I SAY?
HA

...I'M A PERVERT.
...THAT'S WHAT YOU'RE THINKING, ISN'T IT?
I MEAN, AFTER ALL...
IT'S JUST NOT NORMAL FOR A GLOOMY AND PLAIN OFFICE WORKER LIKE ME TO DRESS UP IN SUCH SLUTTY COSTUMES.
BUT... I LIKE IT. I LIKE COSPLAYING... AND I LIKE HAVING MY PICTURE TAKEN.
I WOULD HAVE PREFERRED IT IF NO ONE HAD EVER FOUND OUT... BUT I GUESS IT WAS INEVITABLE.
I SHOULD JUST DIE.
CLENCH
WAAAAH! WAIT A MINUTE!
...I'M TOTALLY THRILLED ABOUT THIS!
WE SHARE THE SAME HOBBY... AND YOU'RE EVEN COSPLAYING A CHARACTER I REALLY LIKE. THAT'S JUST PLAIN AWESOME!
BA-THUMP
きゅん...
YOSHINO-SAN...

バタバタバタッ
THUD THUD THUD
!
バタバタ
THUD THUD
SHIT! SOMEONE'S COMING!
F-FOR NOW, LET'S GET IN A LOCKER!
AHH, SERIOUSLY? IT CAME UNDONE RIGHT NOW?!
SHOVE!
I SHOULDN'T HAVE RUSHED TO FINISH IT!
ドキ
BA-THUMP
ドキ
BA-THUMP
BA-THUMP
ドキ

PRESS
!
SHIT... IF SHE KEEPS PRESSING UP AGAINST ME LIKE THAT...!
PANIC
PREEEESS
AH ...
BA-THUMP
PRESS
!
KA-CHAK
THUD THUD THUD
!
LOOKS LIKE SHE'S GONE...

CREAK
U-UM...
MOMOI-SAN...?
FIDGET
FIDGET
FIDGET
BA-THUMP
YOUR COCK... WAS ROCK HARD... JUST NOW.
BA-THUMP
I... TURNED YOU ON... DIDN'T I?
BA-THUMP
CREAK
HEY...
YOU CAN'T... GO OUT IN PUBLIC LIKE THAT, CAN YOU?
I'LL... TAKE CARE OF IT FOR YOU.

TAKE CARE... OF IT?
KA-CHINK
WAH!
M-MOMOI-SAN?!
KA-CHINK
TUG!
YOU'RE SO BIG AND HARD...
RUB
AND YOUR TIP IS DRIPPING WITH JUICE... ♥
SHLUP
SHLUP
RUB
RUB
RUB

TREMBLE
TH-THIS IS ALL LIKE A DREAM.
MOMOI-SAN IS RUBBING MY DICK.
AND SHE'S STILL IN COSTUME!
GULP
LIFT
PAUSE
WAH ?!
FLASH!
GASP
PALE
SHIT ...
IT WAS SO EROTIC THAT I JUST KIND OF PICKED UP MY CAMERA!

HMM?
SO YOU LIKE CAMERA VOYEURISM, YOSHINO-SAN?
HUH? UH, NO.
THAT JUST KINDA HAPPEN-ED...
TUG
IT'S ALL RIGHT... DON'T HOLD BACK.
TAKE EVEN MORE DIRTY PICTURES OF ME...
FLUMP!
WAAAH?!
MMPH
MM
SHLUP
SHLUP
MMPH
SHLUP
SHLUP
SHLUP

WAH!
IT'S HOT INSIDE HER MOUTH. IT FEELS SO GOOD!
SLURP
SHUDDER
SLURP
IT'S LIKE I'M MELTING FROM THE WAIST DOWN.
SLURP
HAA
TREMBLE
HA
TREMBLE
MMPH.
SLURP
FLASH!
SLURP
MMPH...
SUCK
MM...
FLASH!
FLASH!
SLUUUUUURP
...!
GAH... M-
SHUDDER SHUDDER
MOMOI-SAN!
SHUDDER

NN...
YOUR COCK IS TWITCHING LIKE CRAZY.
ARE YOU ABOUT TO COME?
Y-
YES!
THEN... WAIT JUST A MOMENT.
GUUH ?!
SHLUD
CREAK
COME...
INSIDE OF ME... ♥
SPREAD
DRIP ♥

HAA
HA
NN...
A LITTLE LOWER ...
PRESS
SQUELCH
YES, LIKE THAT...
SQUELCH
THRUST!
AHHN!
IT WENT IN!

UH... AHH!
THRUST
AH
AHN HAAN♥
YOUR PUSSY'S SO TIGHT!
IT'S LIKE... YOU'RE GOING TO SQUEEZE ME DRY!
AAHH
THRUST THRUST
SQUEEZE
SQUEEZE
AAAHHHH!
YO... SHINO-SAN!
FWAP!
HARDER!
FWAP!
GO... DEEPER!
TREMBLE
FWAP!
TREMBLE
FWAP!

THRUST
AHAA
...
AHH.
THRUST
NNGAAAAH!
THRUST
!
GRAB
SHUDDER
WAH...!
SHUDDER
SHUDDER
NO...
GRODE
RUB
RUB
MY NIPPLES... ARE SO SENSITIVE!
SHLUP!
SHLUD
SQUEEZE
TUG!
UH!
MOMOI... SAN, I'M GONNA...
COOOOOOME!
SHUDDER

AAAHHH!
ALL... YOUR SPERM...
...IS FILLING ME UP!
SPURT
SPURT
SPURT

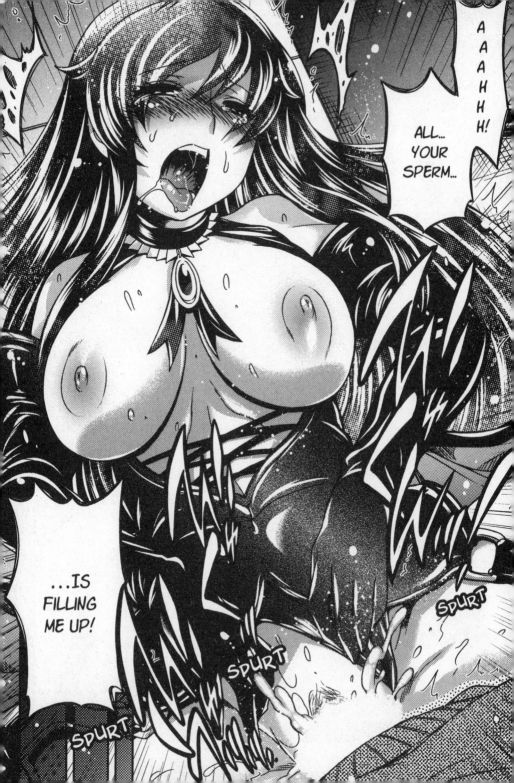

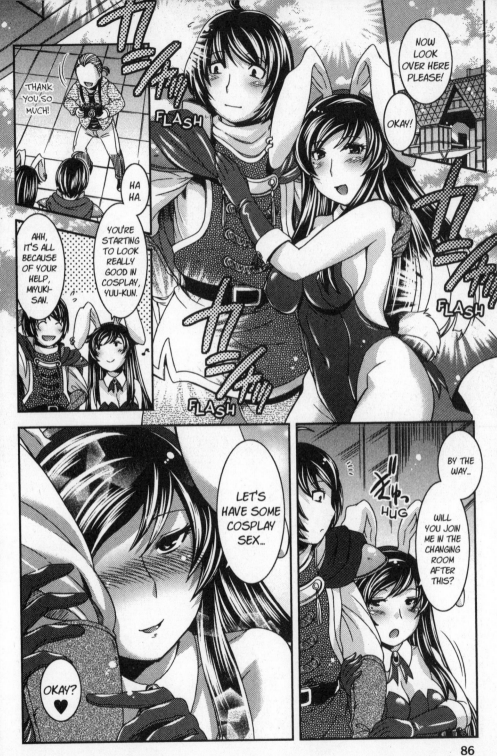

NOW LOOK OVER HERE PLEASE!

OKAY!

THANK YOU SO MUCH!

HA HA.

AHH, IT'S ALL BECAUSE OF YOUR HELP, MIYUKI-SAN.

YOU'RE STARTING TO LOOK REALLY GOOD IN COSPLAY, YUU-KUN.

FLASH

FLASH

FLASH

LET'S HAVE SOME COSPLAY SEX...

OKAY? ♥

BY THE WAY...

WILL YOU JOIN ME IN THE CHANGING ROOM AFTER THIS?

HUG

86

THUD THUD THUD THUD
ARRRRRRRGH, NANA-MIIII!
THUD
SHOVE!
SIS♥COS
WHAT, ANII? YOU JUST CAME BARGING IN HERE YELLING...
AND WOULD IT KILL YOU TO KNOCK?
DON'T. PLAY. DUMB!
YOU DELETED LAST WEEK'S "MAGICAL MAIDEN RIRUHA ★ RIRURA," DIDN'T YOU?!
GULP

THAT SHOW IS FULL OF BITS THAT CAN'T BE UNDER-STOOD FROM JUST ONE WATCHING.
SO YOU HAVE TO WATCH EACH EPISODE AT LEAST TEN TIMES.
TREMBLE
TREMBLE TREMBLE
I'D ONLY WATCHED THAT ONE TWICE, AND YOU...!!
WAAAAAAHH
AHHHH, SHUT UP!
SHOVE
IT'S JUST ANIME. WHAT ARE YOU GETTING SO WORKED UP FOR? IT'S SO DUMB!
WHOA!
HEY.
WAIT...
GET OUT!
SHOVE
SHOVE
NANAMI!
CLICK
SLAM!
HEY, NANAMI!
THUD
THUD THUD
I'M NOT DONE TALKING TO YOU!
ARGH, DAMN NANAMI.
SHE WAS SO CUTE WHEN SHE WAS LITTLE...

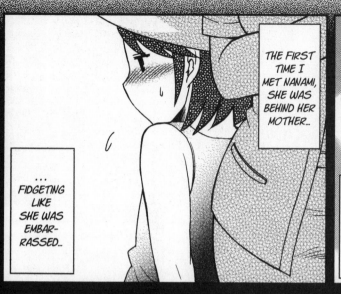

MY DAD REMARRIED WHEN I WAS IN JUNIOR HIGH...

...AND I GOT A NEW MOM AND SISTER.

THE FIRST TIME I MET NANAMI, SHE WAS BEHIND HER MOTHER...

...FIDGETING LIKE SHE WAS EMBARRASSED...

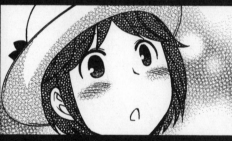

OHH, SO YOU'RE NANAMI?!

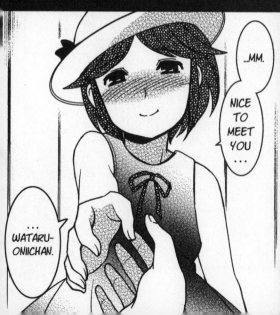

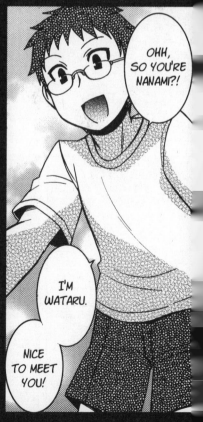

...MM.

NICE TO MEET YOU...

I'M WATARU.

NICE TO MEET YOU!

...WATARU-ONIICHAN.

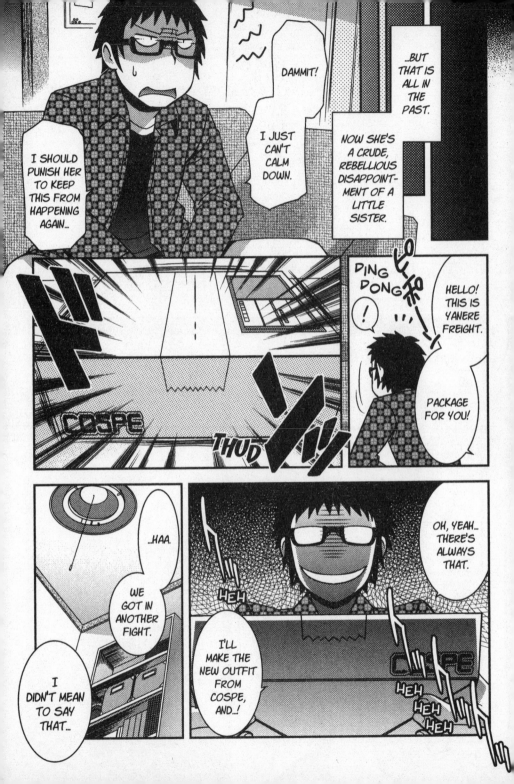

I SHOULD PUNISH HER TO KEEP THIS FROM HAPPENING AGAIN...

DAMMIT!

I JUST CAN'T CALM DOWN.

...BUT THAT IS ALL IN THE PAST.

NOW SHE'S A CRUDE, REBELLIOUS DISAPPOINTMENT OF A LITTLE SISTER.

DING DONG

!

HELLO! THIS IS YANERE FREIGHT.

PACKAGE FOR YOU!

CoSPE

THUD

...HAA.

WE GOT IN ANOTHER FIGHT.

I DIDN'T MEAN TO SAY THAT...

OH, YEAH... THERE'S ALWAYS THAT.

I'LL MAKE THE NEW OUTFIT FROM COSPE, AND...!

CoSPE

HEH

HEH
HEH
HEH

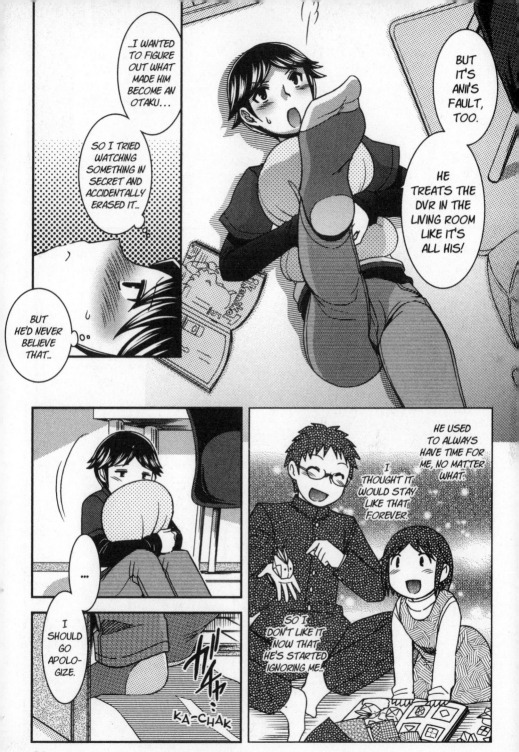

...I WANTED TO FIGURE OUT WHAT MADE HIM BECOME AN OTAKU...

SO I TRIED WATCHING SOMETHING IN SECRET AND ACCIDENTALLY ERASED IT...

BUT HE'D NEVER BELIEVE THAT...

BUT IT'S ANII'S FAULT, TOO.

HE TREATS THE DVR IN THE LIVING ROOM LIKE IT'S ALL HIS!

...

I SHOULD GO APOLO-GIZE.

HE USED TO ALWAYS HAVE TIME FOR ME, NO MATTER WHAT.

I THOUGHT IT WOULD STAY LIKE THAT FOREVER.

SO I DON'T LIKE IT NOW THAT HE'S STARTED IGNORING ME!

ZII!! AP... KA-CHAK.

...HUH?
LIKE I SAID!
I'LL FORGIVE YOU IF YOU ACT OUT THE EVENTS OF THAT EPISODE.
PUT ON THIS OUTFIT!
THIS WAS SUPPOSED TO BE A COLLECTORS' ITEM, BUT THIS IS SPECIAL!
YOU'LL BE RIRUHA!
AND I'LL BE THE BAD GUY!
TADA
AND I'LL RECORD IT FOR POSTERITY WITH THIS CAMERA...
LUCKILY, YOU'RE JUST THE RIGHT SIZE FOR THE CHARAC-TER.
L-
LIKE I WOULD EVER DO WHAT YOU SAY!
YOU CAN NEVER GET BACK SOMETHING THAT'S GONE.
UGH!
...FINE.
I JUST HAVE TO DO IT, RIGHT?!

CAMERA, CHECK!
PROPS, CHECK!
ANII ...
I HAVE IT ON...
OH, THEN LET'S GET STARTED ...
?!
H-
HAS NANAMI ALWAYS BEEN THIS SEXY?!
EVEN IF IT'S PARTLY BECAUSE SHE'S IN COSPLAY...
RUSTLE
...IT STILL GETS ME RIGHT THERE.

O-OH YEAH. THIS ANIME...
HAD A LOT OF SEXY SCENES, DIDN'T IT?
DO I HAVE TO DO THOSE, TOO?
...O-
OF COURSE.
OTHER-WISE IT WOULDN'T BE A PUNISHMENT!
WAAAH!
GRAB
AH...!
HEH... HEH HEH HEH.
AND LAST WEEK THEY PUSHED THE LIMITS OF WHAT THEY COULD ACTUALLY SHOW, TOO.
CLENCH
CLENCH
JUST LIKE THIS, THE TENTACLES...
WERE WRITHING ALL OVER RIRUHA'S ARMS AND LEGS.
SLIIIDE
WAAAAH!

THEN FINALLY THEY DOVE UNDER HER CLOTHING …
…AND STARTED GOING RIGHT FOR HER MOST SENSITIVE AREAS.
RUMMAGE
WAAAH!
AHH.
SQUISH
SQUISH
ANII…
SQUEEZE
PULL
WAAAAAAH!
AND THEN IT PULLED UP HER PANTIES, GIVING HER EXTREME CAMEL TOE!
TUG
PUUUULL
HAAAAAAHN!

SQUIRT
TUG
SQUIRT
HEY, YOU DON'T HAVE TO ACT OUT THE INCONTINENCE PART. THAT'S A LITTLE TOO REALISTIC...
TUG TUG
HAA
HA
HAA
N-NO...
IT'S NOT PEE...
!
YOU DON'T MEAN, SHE...?
AHH!
YANK
NOOOO... DON'T... LOOK.
TWITCH
TWITCH
WAAAAAAAHHH
IT'S EMBAR-RASSING!

BA-THUMP
NANAMI'S SCENT...
THIS IS BAD.
A- ANII ...?!
NANAMI'S SCENT...
AND IT'S SMASHING SOMETHING THAT MAKES ME A HUMAN BEING TO BITS.
LIKE MY REASON, OR MY MORALS, OR SOMETHING LIKE THAT...
WAAAAH!
LUNGE
NO... THAT'S ... DIRTY!
GASP
YOU WERE ALL SMOOTH DOWN HERE WHEN YOU WERE A KID...
BUT NOW YOU'RE ALL GROWN UP, AREN'T YOU?
GASP
DUMB-ASS!
SLURP
DON'T... KEEP...
SHLUP
... STARING LIKE THAT!

SUUUUUCK
HA...!
AH.
SQUIIIIRT
SHUDDER!
AAAAAAHHHHHH!
SHUDDER!
TREMBLE!
HAA...
HA
HAA...
...!
...OH.
SLIDE
SHOW ME YOURS, TOO...
JUST ME DOING THIS...
ISN'T FAIR.
STARE

!
HAA ♡
HAA ♡
WAAAH. IT'S SO BIG...
SPROING!
MM... ♥
SMOOCH
HA... NANA-MII...
MM
MMMPH ...
MM...
MMMPH
MMPH. ♥
MMPH
SHUDDER
SLURP
SLURP
MM ♡

MMMPH...
HAA... MM.
MMMM-MMPH. ♥
SUCK
SUCK
SUCK
SHLUP
SHLUP
SHLUP
SHLUP
SHLUP
LIIICK
HA HA...
THE TIP'S ALL WET.
NOW WE'RE EVEN... ♥
SHLUP
HAA
... NANA-MI...
HA
I... UH... WANT TO...

...YEAH.
IT'S... OKAY.
GO AHEAD. ♥
SHHHLUD
NN
RUB
HAA!
RUB
HA... UH.
PRESS
NNGUH ...
PRESS
THRUST!
THUNK!
HAAAAA!

AHHHN!
AHHH!
SHUDDER
SHLUP
SHLUP
SHLUP
HAAAA!
NANAMI... ARE YOU OKAY?
THRUST
THRUST
YEAH ...
I'M... FINE.
HA
HA
HA
GO DEEPER!
CLENCH
SQUELCH
SQUELCH
SQUELCH
SQUELCH
CLENCH

HA
THIS CAN'T BE REAL...
HAA
I'M HAVING SEX WITH NANAMI.
HA
SHE WAS ALWAYS JUST FAMILY.
SHE WAS ALWAYS JUST A KID.
SHE WAS ALWAYS JUST MY LITTLE SISTER.
THAT'S WHAT I THOUGHT.
... ONII-CHAN.
FWAP
FWAP
FWAP
NANAMI'S... ALWAYS LOVED YOU.
SINCE I FIRST MET YOU...
EVEN NOW! ALWAYS ...
... LOVED YOU!

HAA!
...
SQUIRT
NANA-MIIII!
SPURT!
ONII... CHAAAAAN!
DRIIIIP
SPURT
SPLURT
SPLURT

NNGUH ...
HAA...
AH...
ONII-CHAN ...
CAN I... KISS YOU?
SMOOCH
MM... ♥

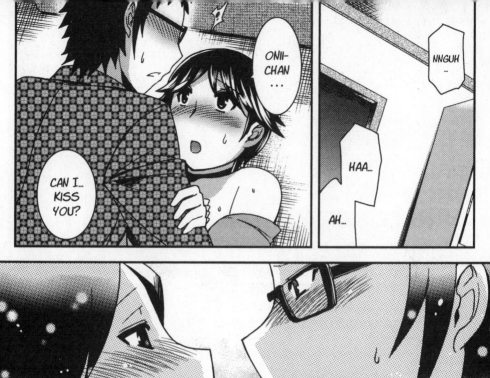

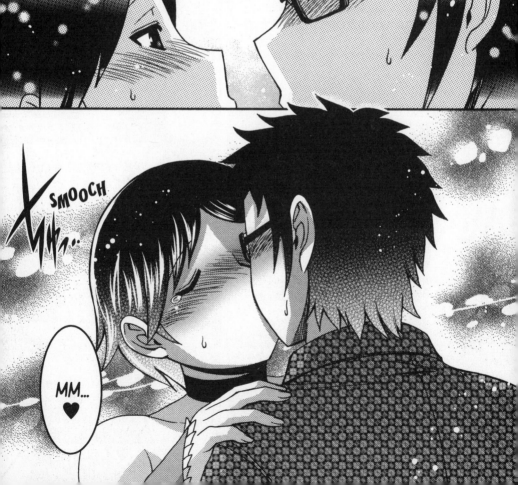

A FEW DAYS LATER...
THUD THUD THUD THUD THUD
HEY, ANII!
WH-WH-WH-WHAT THE HELL IS THIS ?!
TADA!
OHHH...
WELL I JUST CAN'T KEEP SUCH A WONDERFUL VIDEO ALL TO MYSELF, NOW CAN I?
NO... THAT'S ...
DIRTY!
DON'T WORRY ABOUT IT. I ALTERED THE FACE AND THE VOICE.
SLURPING RIRUHA-TAN'S PUSSY! (^ω^)
(ﾟ∀ﾟ) o彡ﾟ TITS!
WHAT A MASTERPIECE.
SWITCH WITH ME MASTER U-P!11
JUST TAKE A LOOK AT ALL THESE ENVIOUS COM-MENTS!
RIGHT NOW THEY'RE PROBABLY ALL GRINDING THEIR TEETH WHILE THEY JACK OFF...
MENACE
MENACE
SMACK
ANII, YOU DUMBASS!
EEEEK!
WHACK
N-N-NO VIOLENCE!

SIS ♥ COS ■ END

COSPLAY♥SISTERS
CostteSisters
ANII, HURRY UP!
IT ALREADY STARTED!
UGGGGHH...
ふわぁ...
SIGH
I SHOULDN'T HAVE STAYED UP ALL NIGHT GOING THROUGH MY GAME COLLECTION.
I'M EX-HAUSTED...
potatos

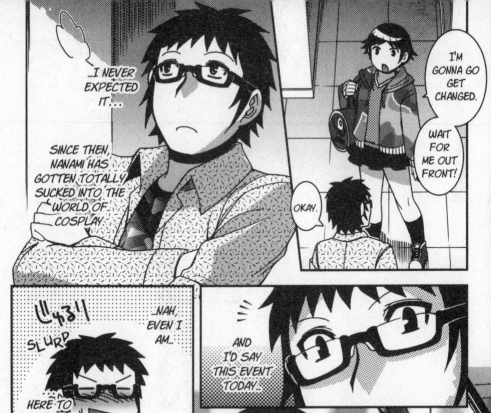

...I NEVER EXPECTED IT...

SINCE THEN, NANAMI HAS GOTTEN TOTALLY SUCKED INTO THE WORLD OF COSPLAY.

I'M GONNA GO GET CHANGED.

WAIT FOR ME OUT FRONT!

OKAY.

SLURP

...NAH, EVEN I AM...

HERE TO TAKE ALL SORTS OF PICTURES OF THE COSPLAYERS.

AND I'D SAY THIS EVENT TODAY...

THERE'S A LOT OF COSPLAYERS HERE TODAY.

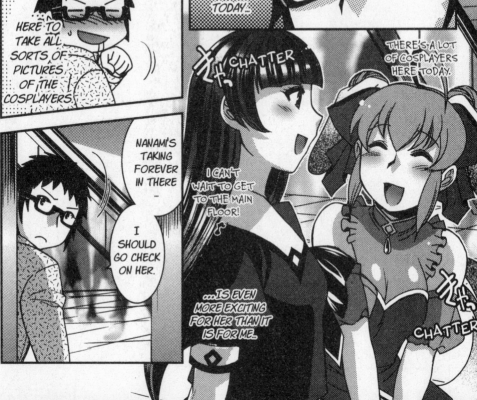

NANAMI'S TAKING FOREVER IN THERE...

I SHOULD GO CHECK ON HER.

CHATTER

I CAN'T WAIT TO GET TO THE MAIN FLOOR!

...IS EVEN MORE EXCITING FOR HER THAN IT IS FOR ME...

CHATTER

PANIC
WH- WHAT SHOULD I DO?
I CAN'T JUST WALK IN THERE...
PANIC
HEY, NANAMI!
WHAT ARE YOU DOING? HURRY UP AND GO GET CHANGED.
!!
BA-THUMP!
A-ANII, SHHH!
THUD
MMMPH?!
WHAT'S WITH YOU? IS THERE SOME KIND OF PROB-LEM?
GASP
...LOOK.

PEEK
?!
AH.
HA HA... YOU'RE SO ADORABLE, YUU-KUN.
THAT COSTUME LOOKS WONDERFUL ON YOU. ♥
SHLUP
WAH!
SHLUP
SHLUP
M- MIYUKI... SAN.
SHLUP
SHLUP
SHLUP
SHLUP
THIS IS EMBARRASSING!
SQUEEZE
SQUEEEEZE
BEING... TIED UP WITH A RIBBON LIKE THIS!

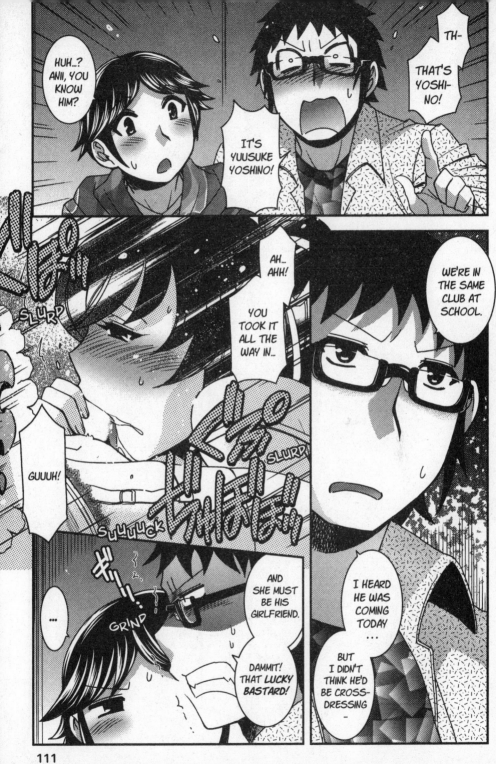

HUH...? ANII, YOU KNOW HIM?

IT'S YUUSUKE YOSHINO!

TH- THAT'S YOSHI-NO!

AH... AHH!

YOU TOOK IT ALL THE WAY IN...

SLURP

GUUUH!

SUUUUCK

SLURP

WE'RE IN THE SAME CLUB AT SCHOOL.

...

GRIND

AND SHE MUST BE HIS GIRLFRIEND.

DAMMIT! THAT LUCKY BASTARD!

I HEARD HE WAS COMING TODAY...

BUT I DIDN'T THINK HE'D BE CROSS-DRESSING...

SLUUUUUURD
WAAAAAH,
AHH!
SHUDDER
AAAAAAHHH!
SHUDDER SHUDDER
NN... HA...
YOUR COCK IS THROB-BING...
SQUISH
CREAK
DOES IT HURT, YUU-KUN?
SHLUP
DO YOU... WANT TO PUT IT IN MY PUSSY?

HAA
... YESSS
I... WANT TO COME...
HA
... INSIDE OF YOU!
HEH.
... GOOD BOY. ♥
AAAHHHH!
THRUST!
...IT'S LIKE I'M DOING A GIRL.
IT GIVES ME THE SHIVERS. ♥
GRIND
AHHH. WAAAGH.
GRIND
SQUELCH
SQUELCH
AAHH ...
MM... ♥
SMOOCH

AH ♥
WHOA ...
AHHN
SO THEY FINALLY PUT IT IN.
AAAHH ♥♥
THAT'S WAY TOO EROTIC ...
...
HAA
GLANCE
HAA
WAAAAH?!
SQUISH
HEY, WHAT ARE YOU DOING?
そわそわ
GRODE GRODE
DID WATCHING OTHERS HAVE SEX TURN YOU ON?
YOUR PANTIES ARE SOPPING WET.
SHLUP

ANII... NOOO ...
WHAT IF SOMEONE SEES?!
SHLUP
SHLUP SHLUP
WE'LL DEAL WITH THAT WHEN IT HAPPENS.
I'M IN TROUBLE, TOO. I'VE BEEN HARD THIS ENTIRE TIME.
GRAB
WHA ...?!
THRUST
AH, AHH ...
AHH ...!
TRRRREMBLE!

D-DUMBASS...
ANII, YOU PERVERT!
HEH...
AH! ♥
RUMMAGE
SPLURT
SPLURT
SPLURT
I CAN'T BELIEVE YOU!
I DON'T WANT TO HEAR THAT FROM SOMEONE WHO BLEW A GUY WITH ALL HER MIGHT.
AND LOOK AT HOW STIFF YOUR NIPPLES ARE!
SQUEEEEEEZE!
WAAAAAAAH!

HAA.
HAA.
JIGGLE ♥
AH. ♥
JIGGLE ♥
YOUR COCK ... IS EVEN BIGGER THAN NORMAL ... ♥
SQUELCH
SQUELCH
SQUELCH SQUELCH
N-NO MOOORE!
SHUDDER
RUB
LET ME COME ...
RUB ♥
MIYUKI-SAAN!
SHUDDER SHUDDER
SLIDE
...I'LL ALLOW IT. ♥

HAAAA... AH.
I'M BEING FILLED...
WITH YOUR HOT CUM!
SPURT

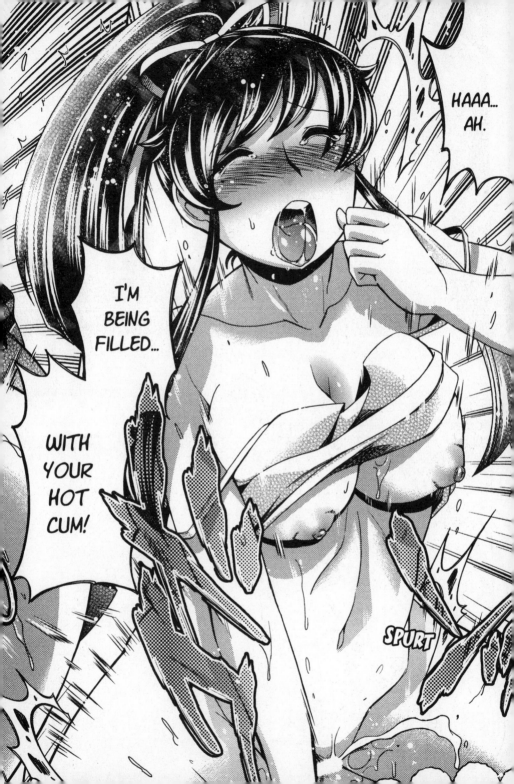

HAA ...
AHH ...
WOBBLE
UNF!
!
CRASH!
SPURT
O- OOTSU ?!
UGH ...
OH... UH...
HI!

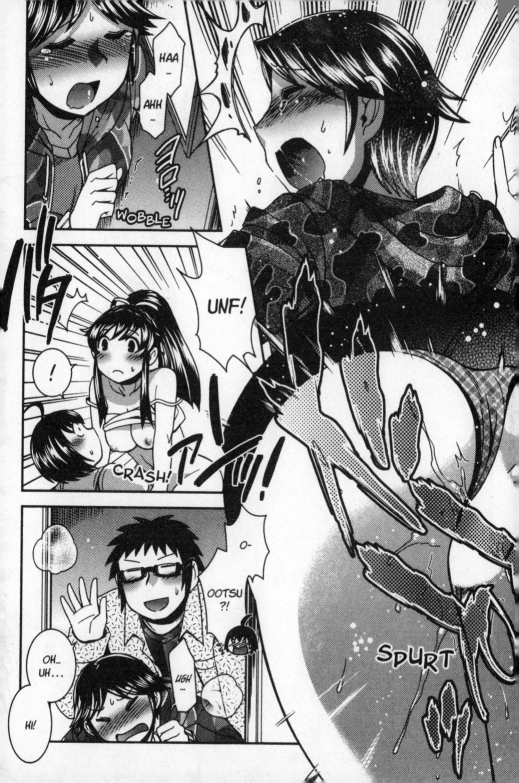

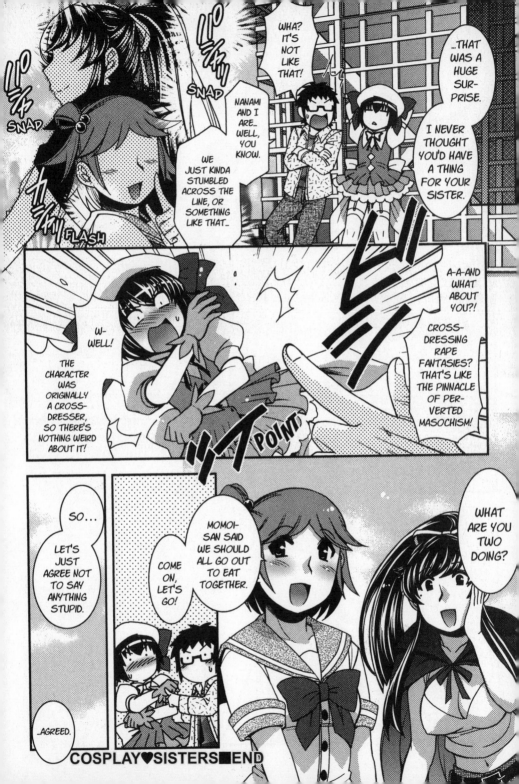

WHA? IT'S NOT LIKE THAT!

...THAT WAS A HUGE SUR- PRISE.

NANAMI AND I ARE... WELL, YOU KNOW.

WE JUST KINDA STUMBLED ACROSS THE LINE, OR SOMETHING LIKE THAT...

I NEVER THOUGHT YOU'D HAVE A THING FOR YOUR SISTER.

SNAP

SNAP

FLASH

A-A-AND WHAT ABOUT YOU?!

W-WELL!

THE CHARACTER WAS ORIGINALLY A CROSS- DRESSER, SO THERE'S NOTHING WEIRD ABOUT IT!

CROSS- DRESSING RAPE FANTASIES? THAT'S LIKE THE PINNACLE OF PER- VERTED MASOCHISM!

POINT

SO...

LET'S JUST AGREE NOT TO SAY ANYTHING STUPID.

COME ON, LET'S GO!

MOMOI- SAN SAID WE SHOULD ALL GO OUT TO EAT TOGETHER.

WHAT ARE YOU TWO DOING?

...AGREED.

COSPLAY♥SISTERS■END

OWW...
I MUST BE GETTING OLD.
THUNK THUNK
I CAN FEEL THE EXHAUSTION BUILDING UP...
RUSTLE
?
HM, WHAT'S THIS?
"REFRESH YOURSELF WITH AROMA-THERAPY AFTER WORKING HARD"...?
REFRESH YOURSELF!
WITH AROMATHERAPY AFTER WORKING HARD ♪
OUR DELUXE LYMPH MASSAGE WILL EASE AWAY YOUR TENSION. ｡(*^_^*)｡
OUR FEMALE STAFF ARE WAITING FOR YOU HERE AT OUR SPARKLING FRESH SHOP.
DO STOP IN FOR A BREAK AFTER WORK!
K-Manek
HMM... IT'S IN THE BACK ALLEY.
I THINK I'LL CHECK IT OUT.

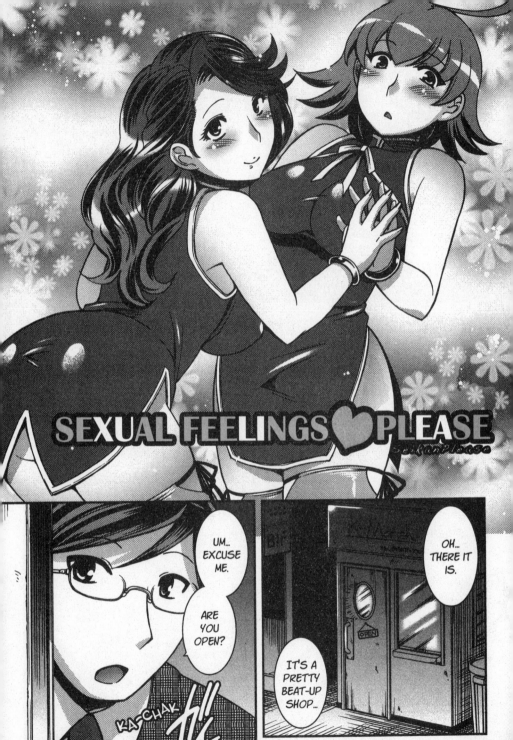

SEXUAL FEELINGS ♡ PLEASE

UM... EXCUSE ME.

ARE YOU OPEN?

OH... THERE IT IS.

IT'S A PRETTY BEAT-UP SHOP...

KA-CHAK

WHOOSH
ROAR!
GO TO **HELL**, YOU DAMN DEBT COLLEC-TOR!
WAAH ?!
FWISH
Y-YOU'VE GOT IT WRONG!
I JUST STOP-PED BY BECAUSE I SAW YOUR FLYER!
FWOOSH
GRIND
WAAAH! IT'S NO USE.
SHE'S NOT LISTENING TO A WORD I SAY!
GRIND GRIND
CLAP!
CLAP!

NINA-CHAN, THAT'S ENOUGH!
!
ARE YOU ALL RIGHT, SIR?
I DO APOLOGIZE FOR WHAT HAPPENED EARLIER.
THINGS ARE RATHER DIFFICULT HERE BECAUSE OF THE RECESSION ...
OH...
BUT REALLY, THIS LOCATION IN THE BACK ALLEY IS THE ABSOLUTE WORST!
NO ONE EVER COMES TO A PLACE LIKE THIS ...
MENACE
NINA-CHAN ...
IF YOU SAY ANYTHING ELSE, I'LL CUT YOUR PAY.
EEK!
IS THIS PLACE REALLY ALL RIGHT?

WELL, THEN. LET'S START WITH THE SHIATSU MASSAGE.
IF YOU HAVE ANY KNOTS THAT YOU'RE WORRIED ABOUT OR IF ANYTHING HURTS, PLEASE DO TELL US.
PRESS
OH...
SQUEEZE
SQUEEZE
KNEAD
KNEAD

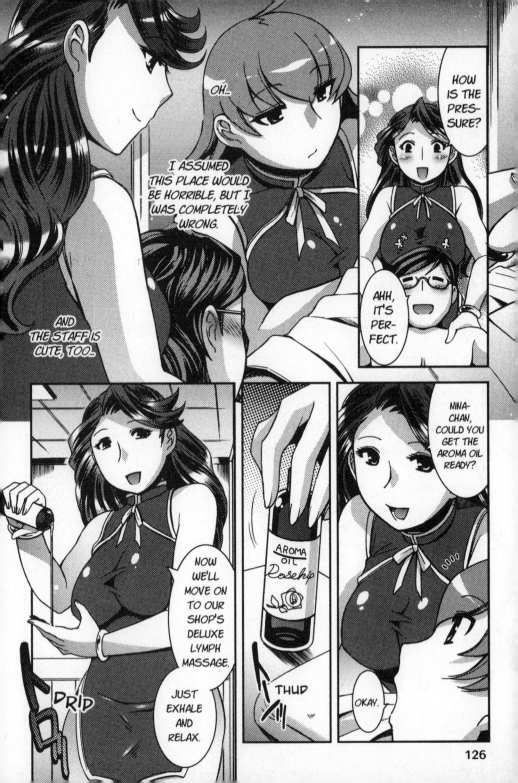

OH...

I ASSUMED THIS PLACE WOULD BE HORRIBLE, BUT I WAS COMPLETELY WRONG.

AND THE STAFF IS CUTE, TOO...

HOW IS THE PRESSURE?

AHH, IT'S PERFECT.

NINA-CHAN, COULD YOU GET THE AROMA OIL READY?

NOW WE'LL MOVE ON TO OUR SHOP'S DELUXE LYMPH MASSAGE.

JUST EXHALE AND RELAX.

AROMA OIL Rosehip

THUD

OKAY.

DRIP

126

SHLOOP
O-
OOOHHH ?!
SHLID
SHLOOP
SHLOOP
SHLID
SHLID
UGH... TH-THIS IS!
RUB
THEIR FINGERS ARE SLIPPERY WITH OIL AND RUBBING ALL OVER MY BODY...
RUB
THIS IS BAD!
!
SWELL!

H-HEY!
WHAT ARE YOU GETTING ALL WORKED UP FOR?!
BLUSH
IT'S AN INVOLUNTARY REACTION...
UH ...
I-I'M SORRY.
...
SIR, IT LOOKS LIKE YOU'RE QUITE STRESSED.
SMILE
WE'LL WORK SOME OF THAT OFF WITH OUR SHOP'S ORIGINAL VIP COURSE. ♥
WH-WHAAAA?!
KURO-KAWA-SAN, YOU DON'T MEAN..?
OH? IS THERE A PROBLEM WITH THAT?

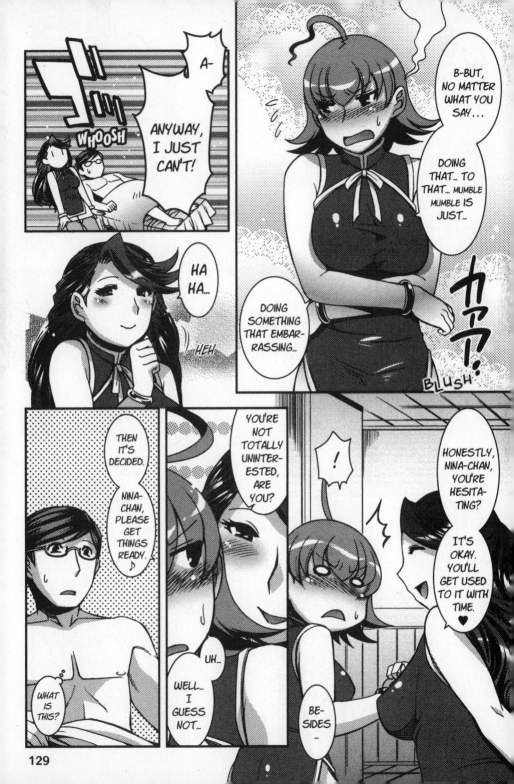

WHOOSH

A- ANYWAY, I JUST CAN'T!

HA HA... HEH.

B-BUT, NO MATTER WHAT YOU SAY...

DOING THAT... TO THAT... MUMBLE MUMBLE IS JUST...

DOING SOMETHING THAT EMBARRASSING...

KAAA?!

BLUSH

THEN IT'S DECIDED.

NINA-CHAN, PLEASE GET THINGS READY. ♪

WHAT IS THIS?

YOU'RE NOT TOTALLY UNINTERESTED, ARE YOU?

UH...

WELL... I GUESS NOT...

!

HONESTLY, NINA-CHAN, YOU'RE HESITATING?

IT'S OKAY. YOU'LL GET USED TO IT WITH TIME. ♥

BE-SIDES...

129

OKAY.
NOW WE'LL RUB YOUR ROCK HARD, SWOLLEN PLACE UNTIL IT SUBSIDES. ♥
SQUISH
OH...
RUB
GUH ...
SQUISH
WHOOOOOOOA!
RUB
RUB
RUB

I-I NEVER IMAGINED I'D GET TO EXPERIENCE A DOUBLE TITTY FUCK!
SHUDDER
THAT SHIVER THAT RUNS THROUGH ME WHEN THEY RUB THE UNDERSIDE WITH THEIR NIPPLES...
THE HAPPINESS OF BEING WRAPPED IN TAUT BREASTS...
SHUDDER
GUUUH, IT'S JUST TOO MUCH!
UHH... IT'S TWITCHING ...
SQUISH
SQUISH
COME ON, NINA-CHAN. USE YOUR MOUTH, TOO.
HUH?
AH.
O-OKAY ...
SLURP

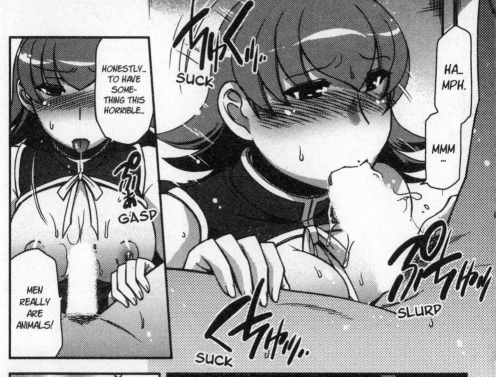

HONESTLY... TO HAVE SOMETHING THIS HORRIBLE...

GASP

MEN REALLY ARE ANIMALS!

SUCK

SLURP

SUCK

HA... MPH.

MMM...

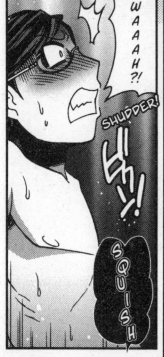

WAAAH?!

SHUDDER!

SQUISH

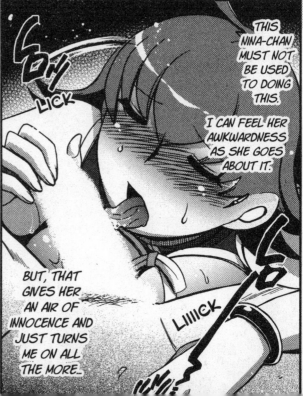

LICK

THIS NINA-CHAN MUST NOT BE USED TO DOING THIS.

I CAN FEEL HER AWKWARDNESS AS SHE GOES ABOUT IT.

BUT, THAT GIVES HER AN AIR OF INNOCENCE AND JUST TURNS ME ON ALL THE MORE...

LIIIICK

WH-WHOA!
SQUISH
SHE'S MAS-SAGING MY BALLS ?!
KNEAD KNEAD
SLUUUURD
AAAAHH! NO WAY...
SHE'S SUCKING ON THE HEAD OF MY DICK AT THE SAME TIME. SHIT!
HEY... HOW... IS IT?
DOES IT FEEL GOOD?
SLURP SLURP
E-EVEN IF SHE ASKS...
IT FEELS SO GOOD I CAN'T EVEN TALK!
KNEAD KNEAD KNEAD
!!!
SPLURT
SPLUUUURT

HAA...
SHUDDER
WOW... IT SMELLS LIKE SEX.
MY HEAD'S... GETTING FUZZY. ♥
SHUDDER
GOOD JOB, NINA-CHAN.
AND OUR CUSTOMER ENJOYED HIMSELF, TOO. ♥
KURO-KAWA-SAN...
LOOK... YOU'VE GOT SOME ON YOUR FACE.
AH...
WE HAVE TO GET YOU CLEAN... ♥
LICK
U-UM...
IT SEEMS YOU HAVEN'T WORKED OUT ALL THE "TENSION" YET...
POP UP
COULD YOU TRY A BIT HARDER?
!

HA HA...
IS THAT SO?
IN THAT CASE ...
HOW ABOUT A SUCTION MASSAGE?
TUG
GULP
O-OKAY, THEN.
I WON'T HOLD BACK!
THRUST!
HAAAN!

NNGAAH... ♥
THRUST
A-AMAZING.
I CAN FEEL IT UP IN MY WOMB!
THRUST
THRUST
...
AHHN.
...KUROKAWA-SAN LOOKS LIKE SHE FEELS REALLY GOOD...
SHUDDER!
I-I WANT THAT, TOO!
AH! ♥
AH.
....! ♥

!
...SIR,
COULD YOU DO NINA-CHAN AS WELL?
OH... YES.
SHLUP
HAA!
AH... WAH!
GO... SLOWER!
THRUST!
THRUST
THRUST THRUST

HA HA... NINA-CHAN...
AH
I'LL MAKE YOU FEEL EVER BETTER. ♥
HAA
AHH..!
KURO... KAWA-SAN!
NO! NOT THERE..!
SUCK
NNGH...
NN!
SLURP
SLURP
SLURP
SUCK
HAAAAAH!
UGH...! I'M...
I'M CUMMING...!
SHIVER
THRUST
NOOOOO!
IF YOU DO IT THAT HARD...
I'LL COME!
I'M COOOO-MING!
THRUST
THRUST

HAAAA...!
SPURT
AAHH...
AAAAHHH!
SQUIRT SQUIRT
HAA...
HAA.
TWITCH
YOU SPILLED...
SO MUCH SPERM... INSIDE OF ME... ♥
SHLUP
TWITCH
AHH...
I'VE RELEASED ALL OF MY TENSION THANKS TO YOU.
THANK YOU!

I'M JUST GLAD TO KNOW THAT YOU'RE SATIS-FIED. ♥
¥1,500,000
AND HERE IS THE BILL.
SPLUTTER
WH-WHAT THE HELL IS THIS?!
THE PRICE OF EACH MASSAGE AND VARIOUS OTHER BITS OF AFTER-CARE.
IT'S THE VALUE OF OUR VERY BEST EFFORTS. ♪
L-LIKE I COULD EVER AFFORD THIS!
IF YOU AGREE TO CALL IN NEW CUSTOM-ERS FOR US INSTEAD...
REALLY?!
I SUPPOSE WE COULD CALL IT EVEN.
A FEW MINUTES LATER...
WA HA HA!
YOU LOOK PRETTY GOOD.
OH MY, IT'S WONDER-FUL. ♥
SO NOW WE'LL LEAVE YOU TO IT!
GLOOM
...
IN THE END, I SPENT THE ENTIRE NIGHT...
...ENTICING NEW CUSTOM-ERS IN THIS JOKE OF A COSTUME...
SEXUAL ♥ PLEASE ■ END

TAP
...ALL RIGHT.
AND NOW... IT'S DONE.
GOOD JOB, YAMADA!
THAT WAS TOUGH, WASN'T IT? THANKS SO MUCH!
AHH, IT'S ALL BECAUSE OF YOUR SUPPORT, KUBOTA -SEMPAI.
I WOULD HAVE MISSED THE LAST TRAIN IF I'D BEEN WORKING ALONE.
CREAK
KA-CHAK

HERE, SOME COFFEE.
CHITOSE KUBOTA-SEMPAI IS A HARD-WORKING CAREER WOMAN.
OH, GREAT.
THANKS.
SHE'S A DEPENDABLE PERSON WHO DECIDED TO TAKE ME, THE NEW KID, UNDER HER WING.
BY THE WAY...
WANT TO JOIN ME FOR A DRINK AFTER THIS?
I KNOW A GOOD BAR.
WHAT? YOU DON'T WANT TO DRINK WITH ME?
HMPH
SHAKE SHAKE SHAKE
N-NO! I'D LOVE TO JOIN YOU!
GULP
UH!
HA HA. THAT'S THE SPIRIT! ♥
THERE IS JUST ONE LITTLE PROBLEM WITH HER...

KA-CHAK
UHHH, I'M HOOOME!
IT'S NOT "I'M HOME," SEMPAI.
SHUT
THIS IS MY PLACE ...
... HEY.
HAAAA...
W- WAIT A MINUTE!
DRUNK
PLEASE DON'T SLEEP IN MY ENTRY-WAY!
DRUNKEN HONEY

COME ON. IT'S JUST A LITTLE FURTHER, SO HANG IN THERE!
MWA-AAAAH...
...I MET KUBOTA-SEMPAI AT THE COMPANY WELCOME PARTY.
WHAT WAS THAT "MWAAAH" ABOUT?
I WAS LOOKING AFTER SEMPAI, WHO WAS DEAD DRUNK...
...AND I FOUND OUT THAT WE JUST HAPPENED TO LIVE NEAR THE SAME STATION.
EVER SINCE THEN...
AHHHHH.
I'M SOOO DRUNK!
FLUMP
...SHE USES MY PLACE LIKE A SORT OF HOTEL...
YAMADAAA, WATER...
I'M THIRSTY!
YEAH, YEAH...
HONESTLY... SHE'S SUCH A DEPENDABLE AND GORGEOUS SEMPAI WHEN SHE'S SOBER.
CLUNK
THE DIFFERENCE IS WAY TOO STARK...

SEMPAI, I BROUGHT YOU SOME WATER... OH.
HUH? SHE'S ASLEEP?
ZZZ
ZZZ
JIGGLE
ZZZ
...WH-
WHAT'S WITH HER CLOTHES?!
GULP
BA-THUMP
BA-THUMP
BA-THUMP
CLINK
BA-THUMP
BA-THUMP
BA-THUMP
...
BA-THUMP
BA-THUMP
CREAK

SNUGGLE

UHHH-NGH.

STARTLE

C-C-C-CALM DOWN.

SHE'S YOUR BOSS!

BA-THUMP

FLOP

jiggle

!

IF YOU GO AFTER HER, YOU COULD GET YOUR-SELF FIRED...

BA-THUMP

BA-THUMP

GRAB

...NO.

CREAK

SHE USUALLY JUST POLITELY ROLLS INTO BED.

IF SHE DOES THIS...

WAH...
HER ASS IS MEATY AND HAS SOME ELASTICITY TO IT...
GROPE
GROPE
GROPE
GROPE
IT'S LIKE I'M TOUCHING A PAIR OF BOOBS!
SLIDE
...
TUG
PULL

TH- THIS IS BAD.
IF I KEEP GOING, IT REALLY WON'T BE GOOD.
SLIDE
SLIDE
SLIDE
MY BRAIN KNOWS THAT...
BUT MY HANDS JUST KEEP MOVING!
SLIDE
PLOP
BA-THUMP
...!
I-I FINALLY SAW IT...
SQUISH
SEMPAI'S... SEMPAI'S PUSSY...

HA
HAA
KA-CHINK
HAA
KA-CHINK
KA-CHINK
SPROING!
I'M SORRY, SEMPAI ...
BUT ...
CREAK
I JUST CAN'T HOLD BACK ANY LONGER!
PRESS!

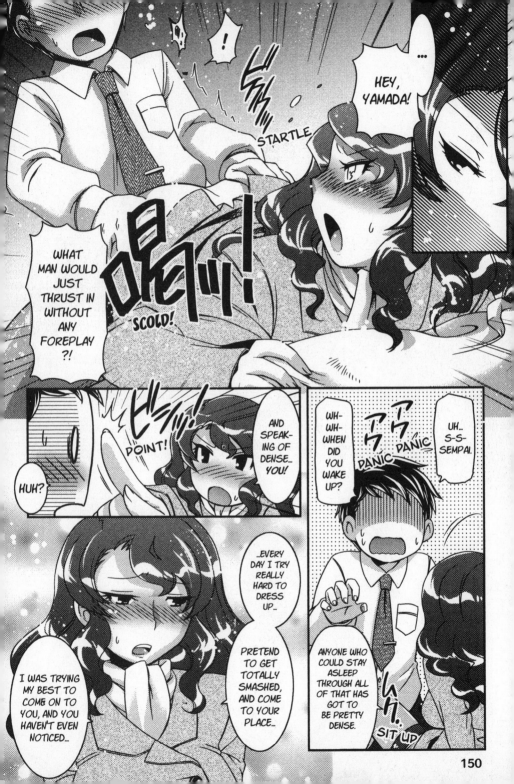

HEY, YAMADA!

...

STARTLE

WHAT MAN WOULD JUST THRUST IN WITHOUT ANY FOREPLAY?!

SCOLD!

AND SPEAKING OF DENSE... YOU!

POINT!

HUH?

...EVERY DAY I TRY REALLY HARD TO DRESS UP...

PRETEND TO GET TOTALLY SMASHED, AND COME TO YOUR PLACE...

I WAS TRYING MY BEST TO COME ON TO YOU, AND YOU HAVEN'T EVEN NOTICED...

WH-WH-WHEN DID YOU WAKE UP?

PANIC PANIC

UH... S-S-SEMPAI.

ANYONE WHO COULD STAY ASLEEP THROUGH ALL OF THAT HAS GOT TO BE PRETTY DENSE.

SIT UP

!
YOU MEAN, SEMPAI HAD THIS IN MIND FROM THE BEGINNING?
?
BLUSH
U-UM, SEMPAI,
I...
!
SMOOCH
...YOU DOLT!
YOU MADE ME WAIT FOR-EVER. ♥
SEMPAI ...

NN...
HONESTLY, YAMADA, YOU LIKE BOOBS WAY TOO MUCH.
GROPE
YOU'VE BEEN GROPING THEM THIS ENTIRE TIME.
GROPE
MEN ARE JUST INSTINCTUALLY ATTRACTED TO THE TWIN MOUNDS.
HMM...
THEN WHICH FEELS BETTER TO TOUCH, MY BOOBS OR MY ASS?
I COULDN'T POSSIBLY CHOOSE.
THEY'RE BOTH PRICE-LESS.
SUCK
AHHN!♥

SHUDDER
HA... AHHN!
SHUDDER
AHH...
SLIDE
SHLUP
!
SHUDDER!
AHH...!
HAA.
SHUDDER!
SHUDDER! SHUDDER!
SHLUP SHLUP
AAAAHHH!
SHLUP SHLUP

AHH...
SHLUP
AH.
SHLUP
SHLUP
SHLUP
HAA.
HAA.
TREMBLE
HAA.
TREMBLE
HAAA...
SHLUP
WAAAH!
SHUDDER
AH... AHH.
RUB
RUB
RUB
HAAAA...!
WAH!
NOOO...
SHLUP
IF YOU... KEEP DOING THAT...!
SHUDDER!
SHUDDER! SHUDDER!
SHLUP SHLUP

...!
SHUDDER
HA AH
SHLUP
HAA
SHUDDER
SHUDDER
HA
...HEY... YAMADAA...
HA
...!
HAA
I WANT IT... YOUR COCK...
TH-THEN...
EXCUSE... ME...
PRESS

NNNGH!
THRUST!
THRUST
THRUST
THRUST
THRUST
HAA... AH.
SO...
FWAP
FWAP
IN-TENSE!
FWAP

!
AH.
AHH ...
THRUST
AAAAHHH..!
THRUST
THRUST
AH. ♥
YOUR PUSSY... IS SQUEEZ-ING ME LIKE CRAZY.
IT'S LIKE IT'S TRYING TO EAT UP MY COCK!
DON'T ...
...TALK LIKE I'M SOME KIND OF ANIMAL! ♥
THRUST THRUST THRUST
THRUST
HA HA
AH
GRAB
SIT UP!
WAAAAH?!

AH...!
SO... DEEP!
IT'S ...
SQUELCH
SQUELCH
SQUELCH
SQUELCH
BUMPING UP... AGAINST MY INSIDES!
S- SEMPAI...
HA
HAA
HA
NN ... ♥
SMOOCH
MMWAAAAH... ♥
SMOOCH
HAA...
THRUST
NN.
NNGH...
THRUST
NNNNNNGH!
THRUST
THRUST

...!
SHUDDER
SEM... PAI, I'M GONNA...!
YEAH... COME!
SHUDDER
POUR IT ALL OUT... INSIDE OF ME!
AHH!
NNGAH!
AAAAAHHH!
SPURT
SPURT

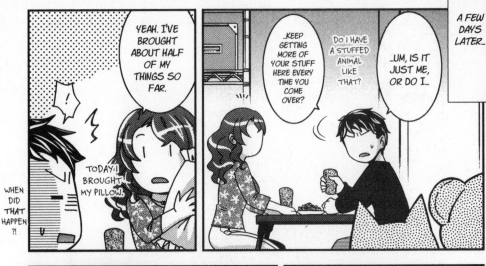

A FEW DAYS LATER...

..UM, IS IT JUST ME, OR DO I...

DO I HAVE A STUFFED ANIMAL LIKE THAT?

..KEEP GETTING MORE OF YOUR STUFF HERE EVERY TIME YOU COME OVER?

YEAH. I'VE BROUGHT ABOUT HALF OF MY THINGS SO FAR.

TODAY I BROUGHT MY PILLOW.

WHEN DID THAT HAPPEN?!

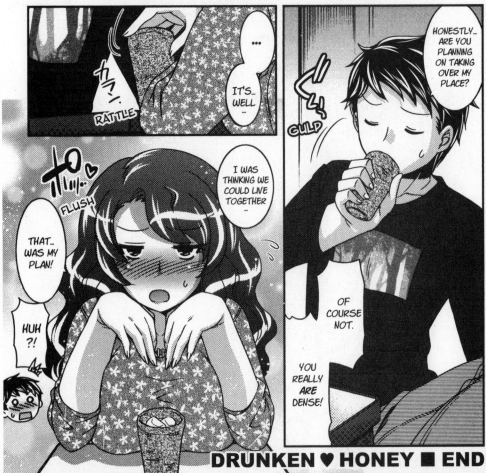

...

IT'S... WELL...

RATTLE

HONESTLY... ARE YOU PLANNING ON TAKING OVER MY PLACE?

GULP

I WAS THINKING WE COULD LIVE TOGETHER...

FLUSH

THAT... WAS MY PLAN!

HUH?!

OF COURSE NOT.

YOU REALLY ARE DENSE!

DRUNKEN ♥ HONEY ■ END

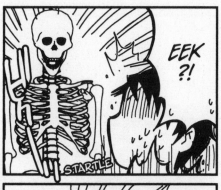

EEK
?!

STARTLE

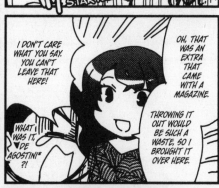

I DON'T CARE WHAT YOU SAY. YOU CAN'T LEAVE THAT HERE!

WHAT WAS IT, DE AGOSTINI* ?!

OH, THAT WAS AN EXTRA THAT CAME WITH A MAGAZINE.

THROWING IT OUT WOULD BE SUCH A WASTE, SO I BROUGHT IT OVER HERE.

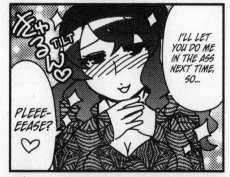

TILT

I'LL LET YOU DO ME IN THE ASS NEXT TIME, SO...

PLEEE-EEASE?
♡

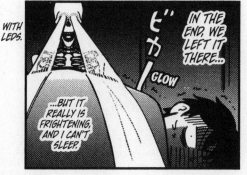

WITH LEDS.

GLOW

IN THE END, WE LEFT IT THERE...

...BUT IT REALLY IS FRIGHTENING, AND I CAN'T SLEEP.

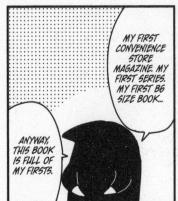

ANYWAY, THIS BOOK IS FULL OF MY FIRSTS.

MY FIRST CONVENIENCE STORE MAGAZINE. MY FIRST SERIES. MY FIRST B6 SIZE BOOK...

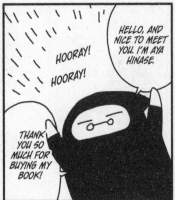

HOORAY! HOORAY!

THANK YOU SO MUCH FOR BUYING MY BOOK!

HELLO, AND NICE TO MEET YOU. I'M AYA HINASE.

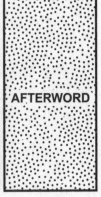

AFTERWORD

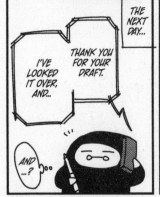

THE NEXT DAY...

THANK YOU FOR YOUR DRAFT.

I'VE LOOKED IT OVER, AND...

AND ...?

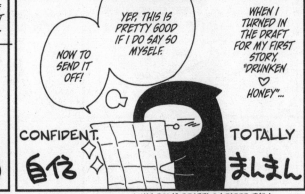

NOW TO SEND IT OFF!

YEP, THIS IS PRETTY GOOD IF I DO SAY SO MYSELF.

WHEN I TURNED IN THE DRAFT FOR MY FIRST STORY, "DRUNKEN ♡ HONEY"...

CONFIDENT. 自信 ◇

TOTALLY まんまん

I WAS DOING DRAFTS ON PAPER THEN.

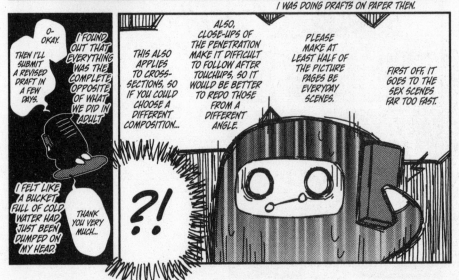

O-OKAY. THEN I'LL SUBMIT A REVISED DRAFT IN A FEW DAYS.

I FOUND OUT THAT EVERYTHING WAS THE COMPLETE OPPOSITE OF WHAT WE DID IN ADULT

THIS ALSO APPLIES TO CROSS-SECTIONS, SO IF YOU COULD CHOOSE A DIFFERENT COMPOSITION...

ALSO, CLOSE-UPS OF THE PENETRATION MAKE IT DIFFICULT TO FOLLOW AFTER TOUCHUPS, SO IT WOULD BE BETTER TO REDO THOSE FROM A DIFFERENT ANGLE.

PLEASE MAKE AT LEAST HALF OF THE PICTURE PAGES BE EVERYDAY SCENES.

FIRST OFF, IT GOES TO THE SEX SCENES FAR TOO FAST.

I FELT LIKE A BUCKET FULL OF COLD WATER HAD JUST BEEN DUMPED ON MY HEAD.

THANK YOU VERY MUCH...

?!

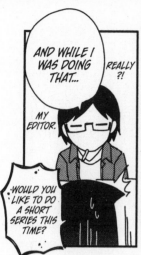

AND WHILE I WAS DOING THAT...

REALLY?!

MY EDITOR.

WOULD YOU LIKE TO DO A SHORT SERIES THIS TIME?

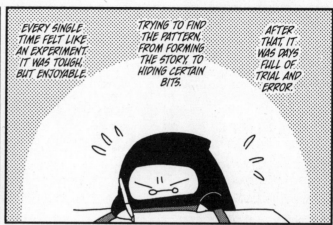

EVERY SINGLE TIME FELT LIKE AN EXPERIMENT. IT WAS TOUGH, BUT ENJOYABLE.

TRYING TO FIND THE PATTERN, FROM FORMING THE STORY, TO HIDING CERTAIN BITS.

AFTER THAT, IT WAS DAYS FULL OF TRIAL AND ERROR.

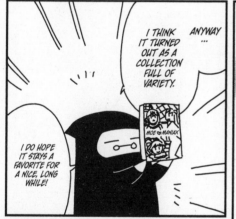

I THINK IT TURNED OUT AS A COLLECTION FULL OF VARIETY.

ANYWAY...

I DO HOPE IT STAYS A FAVORITE FOR A NICE, LONG WHILE!

MOE MANIAX

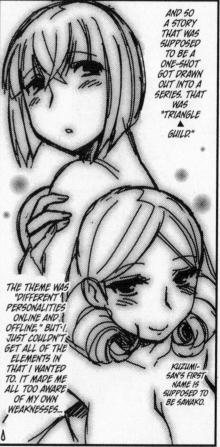

AND SO A STORY THAT WAS SUPPOSED TO BE A ONE-SHOT GOT DRAWN OUT INTO A SERIES. THAT WAS "TRIANGLE ▲ GUILD."

THE THEME WAS "DIFFERENT PERSONALITIES ONLINE AND OFFLINE," BUT I JUST COULDN'T GET ALL OF THE ELEMENTS IN THAT I WANTED TO. IT MADE ME ALL TOO AWARE OF MY OWN WEAKNESSES...

KUZUMI-SAN'S FIRST NAME IS SUPPOSED TO BE SAWAKO.

DIGRESSION NUMBER TWO:

THE REASON ALL OF THE STORIES IN THIS COLLECTION HAVE EITHER ♡ OR △ SYMBOLS IN THEM... ♡ IS BECAUSE AFTER I UNINTENTIONALLY PUT HEARTS IN TWO STORIES, I DECIDED TO JUST MAKE THEM ALL LIKE THAT.

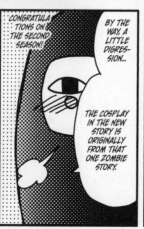

CONGRATULATIONS ON THE SECOND SEASON!

BY THE WAY, A LITTLE DIGRESSION...

THE COSPLAY IN THE NEW STORY IS ORIGINALLY FROM THAT ONE ZOMBIE STORY.

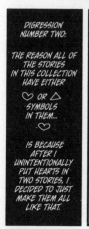

THE END.

Moe ♥ Maniax

もえ♥まに

Aya Hinase

English Edition Published by
PROJECT-H
1487 West 178th Street, Ste. 301
Gardena, CA 90248

First Edition: June 2014
ISBN13: 978-1-62459-130-3
ISBN10: 1-62459-130-2

10 9 8 7 6 5 4 3 2 1
Printed in Canada

CONTENTS

Translation | Leighann Harvey
Lettering | Mharvin Black Castro
Editor | Una Cope
VP Production | MrFred
Sales & Distribution | Yoko Tanigaki

Read digital titles at
www.emanga.com

More hentai for sale at
www.akadot.com

Follow us on Twitter
@projectHbooks

Like us on Facebook
Project-H Books

PROJECT-H

PROJECTH.XXX

PROJECT-H
WWW.PROJECTH.XXX
FOR ALL YOUR HENTAI NEEDS!
English Manga
Japanese Manga
DVD
Photobook
Artbook

PROJECT-H
UNCENSORED
Get your hands on the
Fruitful Body for the special price of only
$17.95!
Fruitful Body
孕みたい彼女
Available NOW at PROJECTH.XXX
*Uncensored Titles Regularly priced at $19.95

Follow us on Twitter
@projectHbooks
Like us on Facebook
Project-H Books
PROJECT-H
HENTAI FESTIVAL 2014
Attend the panel and earn a FREE gift!
10PM - 2AM | July 5th, 2014
LP1 Petree Hall
Anime Expo 2014
LA Convention Center
See girls, play games, win prizes and more!
Follow us on Facebook for exciting updates and special exclusives!
18+ ONLY
AX

DOWNLOAD TO OWN!
AVAILABLE FOR iPAD, KINDLE, NOOK, AND OTHER POPULAR E-READERS! ONLY AT eMANGA!
1000+ TITLES!
SHONEN | SHOJO | YAOI
COMEDY | HENTAI | + MORE!
amazon kindle
kobo
iPad
nook
by Barnes & Noble
android

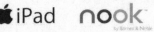

PROJECT-H
PRESENTS
Hard Temptation
UNCENSORED
HARD TEMPTATION
FOR THE SPECIAL PRICE OF
$17.95!
Available NOW at PROJECTH.XXX
*Uncensored Titles Regularly priced at $19.95

Forums are LIVE

PROJECT-H

Recommend titles, vote in polls, make friends & MORE!

Join the Hentai Community
www.forums.projecth.xxx

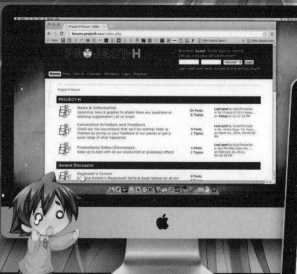

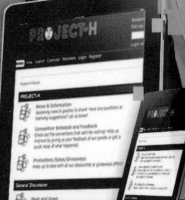

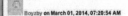

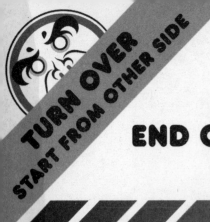

TURN OVER
START FROM OTHER SIDE

THIS IS THE
END OF THE BOOK

This manga was created in its
original hentai format.

WARNING!

Original hentai is read from RIGHT to LEFT!

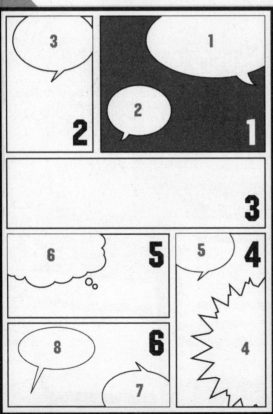

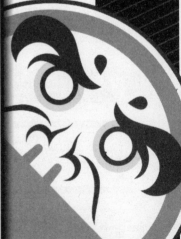